PEACE AGITATOR

the story of
A.J.Muste

W9-COB-505

A. J. goes over the fence at Mead missile base in Nebraska.
Man with mouth open is a reporter. Others are Air Police.

PEACE AGITATOR

the story of A.J.Muste

BY
NAT HENTOFF

INTRODUCTION BY
LARRY GARA

A.J. MUSTE
MEMORIAL INSTITUTE

NEW YORK
1982

This book was originally conceived as a Profile for *The New Yorker* and was then revised and expanded. I am grateful to Mr. William Shawn of *The New Yorker* for permission to use the material that was in the profile.

I am also indebted to the Editorial Board of *Liberation* for permission to quote from articles in that magazine, including A. J. Muste's autobiographical sketches.

First Printing by The Macmillan Company, New York 1963

Second Printing by the A.J. Muste Memorial Institute 1982

Library of Congress Catalog Card Number: 82-71646

ISBN 0-9608096-0-0

Printed in the United States of America

Cover design by Jerry Fargo

Cover photographs courtesy of the War Resisters League

For Jessica, Miranda, Nicholas

TABLE
OF
CONTENTS

TABLE OF CONTENTS

"The horrors which we have seen, the still greater horrors we shall presently see, are not signs that rebels, insubordinate, untameable men, are increasing in number throughout the world, but rather that there is a constant increase, a stupendously rapid increase, in the number of obedient, docile men."

GEORGES BERNANOS

"Peaceableness does not mean trying to disturb nothing or glossing over realities. It is the most profound kind of disturbance we seek to achieve. Nonviolence is not apathy or cowardice or passivity. And the fact that we want peace does not mean that there will not be opposition, suffering, social disorder."

A. J. MUSTE

"The honest man must be a perpetual renegade, the life of an honest man a perpetual infidelity. For the man who wishes to remain faithful to truth must make himself perpetually unfaithful to all the continual, successive, indefatigable, renascent errors."

CHARLES PÉGUY

INTRODUCTION

Reading Nat Hentoff's biography of A.J. Muste has again reminded me how fortunate I was to know A.J. and to work with him in the national office of the Fellowship of Reconciliation during World War II. It was a four-month period between prison stretches for draft resistance, and my job was that of mailing clerk, filling orders for literature from people around the country. A.J. was national secretary of the Fellowship, which meant national director. Although he was clearly the dominant spokesperson for the organization, everyone in the office was treated more like a member of a large family than as a worker with assigned tasks. Pacifists during the war were drawn together by their convictions, and A.J. was simply another one of us, though even then his writings and speeches sometimes reached beyond the ranks of the pacifist community. He seemed to live, breathe and constantly practice nonviolence, on occasion even to the neglect of more mundane matters. He once bought new shoes but was surprised to learn that, in addi-

tion to cash, he would have to supply ration stamps. Here
was a man whose brilliant analyses of world events had impressed us all, yet he was totally unaware of one of the petty
problems that Americans faced during the war.

It was after the war that *Time* Magazine labeled A.J.
"America's No. 1 Pacifist," a title he certainly had earned
by the contributions he had made to the peace movement.
While characterizing any one individual as the number one
pacifist was to oversimplify the issue, A.J. worked in a time
when such recognition resulted from popular support and
acclaim rather than from the kind of media manipulation
later used by television newscasters who designated Jane
Fonda a symbol of anti-Vietnam War protests and Stokely
Carmichael a symbol of Black Power. Muste's was the year
of such radical figures as Norman Thomas, Roger Baldwin
and Scott Nearing, who made outstanding contributions
respectively to democratic socialism, civil liberties and
radical scholarship. Each had a substantial following and
their names suggested the causes with which they were
identified.

Such leadership roles are no longer as clearly defined. In
the 1960s there was much talk in the peace movement
about A.J.'s successor, but it has become clear that the age
of such giants has passed, at least temporarily. Television
reporting, with its emphasis on the present moment,
helped to destroy it. It is worth noting that, despite *Time's*
recognition, a trend towards decentralization in the peace
movement coupled with a growing suspicion of "movement heavies" added to the change away from A.J.'s style.
A.J. was seldom seen on television or interviewed on its
many talk shows, nor was he ever listed in *Who's Who*.

His special skill was as a catalyst in various groups and
organizations. That he could get so many disparate groups
to cooperate in coalition projects was a wonder to behold.

This talent came into special play when he helped to build coalitions against the war in Vietnam, coalitions which included a range of organizations from communist to religious. He also moved many peace organizations to take a more active role in American life, including the Fellowship of Reconciliation, the War Resisters League and various ad hoc action-oriented committees.

The recent trend towards draft resistance has roots in A.J.'s World War II position. First he and some other men, who were over the age for actual service but required by law to register, refused to do so. Then in 1948 he persuaded more than 400 religious leaders and others to sign a complicity statement supporting younger nonregistrants and advising youths to refuse. During the Vietnam era he led the support for those who publicly burned their draft cards, and he continued to publish and speak for total draft refusal. Of course he was joined by many others in this activity but his contributions were major. He played a similar role in the use of nonviolent civil disobedience to protest nuclear weapons and to break down the walls of racial segregation. And he strove always to make radicalism more effective by combining social change with the inner transformation required for a truly liberated society.

Above all, A.J. was a warm human being with a great ability to laugh at himself. But, like everyone else, he had shortcomings. Although he played a vital role in activating numerous organizations, he constantly moved about from one to another. Thus, while he added strength he often failed to provide stability. He always seemed to be searching for the constituency which might develop into the movement he hoped to lead, and one of his major disappointments was the failure of such a movement to appear. While A.J. was ahead of his time on many issues, there were some areas in which he shared the more traditional views of his contemporaries. For example, he was a loving, kind and unselfish husband, but he probably never questioned whether his wife Anna should be more than a helpmate and companion to him. His quotations are full of the terms "mankind" and "man" used to refer to all humans. When the matter of his possible successor in the FOR was discussed, neither he nor any other staff person even considered any of several well-qualified and competent women in the movement. But all of us have been changed by the women's movement and it is unfair to condemn those who lived earlier for not sharing values and practices which only became widely accepted after their time. Had A.J. lived into the 1970s he surely would have been more sensitive to the issue of sexism.

Nat Hentoff's book provides an excellent summary of the life that A.J. led and its reprinting should help to bring his many contributions back into focus. The book captures his personality well: his ability to be authoritative without being autocratic; his emphasis on the politics of nonviolent action; his ability to analyze the world scene and to view it from an international perspective; his humane approach, which frequently led him to abandon a busy schedule in order to counsel a young draft resister or other peace movement worker who was in serious trouble; and finally, his basically religious point of view combined with a way of doing things that enabled the anti-religious to accept him. Nat Hentoff also edited a volume of A.J.'s writings which give the impression of a much more traditional Christian outlook than A.J. projected in person. The emphasis in *Peace Agitator* is correct.

Much has happened since its publication. In 1965 A.J. served as chair of the Fifth Avenue Vietnam Peace Parade

Committee and helped to organize the International Days of Protest Against the Vietnam War. The following year he led a group of peace activists to Saigon where, after a widely-publicized demonstration and press conference, they were deported. He also helped found the National Mobilization Committee to End the War in Vietnam. In 1967, he visited Hanoi where he met Ho Chi Minh. He died shortly thereafter, on February 11, 1967.

Later changes have also affected other people and organizations in this biography. *Liberation* Magazine is no longer published, though its successor *WIN* Magazine (a bi-weekly co-published by the War Resisters League) is still going strong. Bayard Rustin, one of A.J.'s closest followers, still calls himself a pacifist but since 1964 has been director of the A. Philip Randolph Institute and has worked with various labor and liberal political groups rather than with the peace movement. He argued against combining civil rights and antiwar programs, and from time to time has endorsed sending arms and other military aid to Israel. James Farmer has also operated within a more traditional political environment and was for a year Assistant Health, Education and Welfare Secretary under President Nixon. The Congress of Racial Equality, which A.J. helped establish, became caught up in the Black Power, violence vs. nonviolence controversy of the 1960s and finally abandoned nonviolence entirely. Jim Peck, who for years edited CORE's official publication, was fired from that post and soon all white members were excluded from its ranks.

On the other hand, young war resisters continue to be inspired by A.J. Muste's example and writings. They have heard about him from older activists and many know the words so often attributed to him: "There is no way to peace, peace is the way," a quotation, apparently, of a

World War II resistance fighter which A.J. loved to repeat. Now, when the threat of nuclear war looms frighteningly near, the urgency of A.J.'s message is undeniable: "Nonconformity, Holy Disobedience, becomes a virtue, indeed a necessary and indispensable measure of spiritual self-preservation, in a day when the impulse to conform, to acquiesce, to go along, is used as an instrument to subject men to totalitarian rule and involve them in permanent war."

Larry Gara
April 1982

1

THE MAN

*"If I Can't Love Hitler, I Can't Love
at All."*

SINCE HIROSHIMA, the international peace movement
has become bristlingly heterogeneous as it has grown in
numbers through the enlistment of "nuclear pacifists"—
those who had not previously considered pacifism personally or politically plausible until the prospect of a
nuclear war appeared all too possible.

In America, Europe, Asia and Africa, there are more
and more pockets—often small and inchoate, occasionally sizable and disciplined—of agitators for peace. Some
still disavow pacifism as a total personal way of life
while insisting on an end to all armament by nations.
Some support unilateral disarmament by their own
countries; others are convinced that, pragmatically, only
various unilateral "initiatives" can be taken. Some sign
proclamations, attend meetings, and contribute to urgent advertisements in newspapers. Others are direct
actionists—picketing and committing civil disobedience
in the hope of reshaping public opinion.

Although Bertrand Russell is the most widely pub-

1

licized spokesman for an end to the deterrence concept of peace-through-terror, there is no one "leader" of this movement. In fact, sections of it—such as Women Strike for Peace in America—pridefully proclaim that they have hardly any table of organization at all.

There is, however, one man who is more ubiquitous in the widely diverse councils of international peace-makers than any other figure. His own pacifism is absolutist—personal as well as political—but he is able to influence and has achieved the respect of all manner of peace partisans. One reason is his lack of the aggressive self-righteousness which characterizes some of those pacifists who believe only they know the route to unalloyed virtue. A second is his consistent opposition to all armament—of whatever nation and bloc. Another is his record as a resourceful, experienced strategist in the techniques of nonviolent action—in civil rights and labor conflicts in addition to peace campaigns. Furthermore, although the man is soft-spoken and appears gentle, his effect on many has been charismatic. His colleagues in India refer to him as "the American Gandhi."

Abraham Johannes Muste lives in New York, but his travels have made him familiar to peace workers in Europe, India, and Africa. A month before his seventy-eighth birthday on January 8, 1963, he was summoned to India by disciples of Gandhi there. One of the purposes of his visit was to supply advice as to how the teachings of Gandhi could again be made effectual in a country gearing for war against China.

On the way back from India, Muste stopped in England. He attended a conference at Oxford of forty-four nonaligned peace organizations from eighteen countries. The basic intent of the conference was to set up the first world alliance of such independent peace units—by contrast, for example, with the Communist-oriented World

Peace Council. The result was "The International Con-
federation for Disarmament and Peace."

There was also time for Muste to chair a meeting in
London of the World Peace Brigade, an organization
of which he is one of the international co-chairmen.
The main issue on the agenda was the planning of a
"friendship march" from New Delhi to Peking by an
international team of absolutist pacifists who would
protest against violence and preparation for violence on
both sides of the border.

While Muste spends a great deal of his time among
what might be termed professionals of the peace movement throughout the world, he also addresses himself—
whenever he has the opportunity—both to the unconverted and to those who are new to and confused about
the philosophy of nonviolence in an acceleratingly aggressive world. In November, 1959, for example, Muste
was in Accra, Ghana, coordinating an international,
interracial team marching to protest the French decision
to test an atom bomb in the Sahara. Part of his function
was to conduct a workshop on the nature and techniques
of nonviolent resistance for some seventy African volun-
teeds for the team.

One afternoon, a young Ghanian interrupted Muste.
"Now I think I know what nonviolence means," he said
as if lecturing to himself. "It means that if Ghana
should decide to test an atomic bomb, I'd have to op-
pose that most of all."

Muste nodded in pleasure.

In the summer of that year, Muste had been arrested
by Federal authorities for climbing over a barbed-wire
fence into an Atlas missile base near Mead, Nebraska,
thirty miles from Omaha. The demonstration was, first
of all, an attempt to get the widest possible publicity for
this protest against the manufacture of missiles. It was

also an attempt to convince workers at the base of their complicity in an imminent Armageddon.

Muste was one of the leaders of this "Omaha Action, Nonviolence Against Nuclear Policy," a project of the Committee for Nonviolent Action of which Muste is National Chairman. Muste served nine days in jail before trial, and a fine of $500 and a sentence of six months in prison were suspended. Before the sentencing, Muste spoke to the court for some twenty minutes about the aims of Omaha Action. Because of his constant air of inordinately patient reasonableness, Muste is usually chosen as a spokesman in such hostile situations by his fellow actionists. The judge heard him out and seemed impressed by the depth of the elderly man's conviction and the clarity of his ideas.

"Mr. Muste," the judge said, "you should present that argument to Congress, not to this court."

"We are indeed," Muste answered, "but we are seeking to present it to all men as well."

On May 3, 1960, Muste committed civil disobedience again. He helped organize a New York protest against the annual, nationwide, civil defense drill on the grounds that there is no defense against nuclear attack, and that such drills increase the conditioning of governments and their citizens to the possibility of war.

Muste and other pacifists (notably members of *The Catholic Worker,* a newspaper directed by Dorothy Day, who also operates refuges for the poor) had been refusing, since 1955, to take shelter when the sirens sounded; and Muste had been among those jailed in the past. Until 1960, the number of resisters had been small. No doughty group had been larger than the initial twenty-six in 1955. The 1960 demonstration, however, drew an unprecedented one thousand sympathizers to City Hall

Park in downtown New York, and several hundred students demonstrated at colleges throughout the city.

The sharp rise in civil disobedience that May was in part an extension of the still-continuing interest in non-violent action for civil rights among students during the past few years. More and more of them have been gradually applying this doctrine to antiwar activities as well. As one Negro youngster in a 1962 picket line in front of the Atomic Energy Commission office in New York explained, "What's the sense of being integrated into oblivion?"

This merging of forces has, of course, been encouraged by Muste. "If the civil rights movement is to work for fundamental change," he has often urged, "it has to link up with the movement against war."

Also contributing to the size of the 1960 demonstration at City Hall Park had been relentless organizing by a cadre of young mothers who were newcomers to the peace movement. The conversion of mothers to nuclear pacifism has steadily continued—as is most clearly illustrated by the expansion of Women Strike for Peace.

In that May, 1960, protest, more than five hundred remained in the park after the police had delivered a final warning to go underground; and of those who stayed, twenty-six were arrested at random. Muste, though cheerfully conspicuous at the center of the demonstration, was not arrested. The protest, the War Resisters League newsletter happily reported, was "the biggest civil disobedience peace action" in modern American history.

Muste, a member of the executive committee of the War Resisters League, had been treasurer of the Civil Defense Protest Committee coordinating the mass resistance at City Hall Park. He also quickly became treasurer of the Provisional Defense Committee for the luckless twenty-six who were each sentenced to five days in jail.

The proliferating multiplicity of Muste's functions was characteristic. Muste's name is on the letterhead of nearly every American peace organization, provisional and vintage, as well as on those of numerous international pacifist groups. "When you see A.J.'s name," one impatient peace worker has observed, "it's a guarantee of action. He makes things happen." Bradford Lyttle, a fierce young pacifist who has helped direct several major projects of the Committee for Nonviolent Action, adds: "A.J. is the spiritual chairman of every major pacifist demonstration in the country and often is the actual chairman. He's the number one peacemaker in America."

As a further example of Muste in action, there was a confrontation a couple of years ago—at Muste's request —between him and Lieutenant General C. R. Huebner, New York State Director of Civil Defense. The meeting took place at the latter's headquarters in New York City. In evident perplexity, the general watched the arrival of the tall, spindly, white-haired Mr. Muste and a small delegation of peace agitators. A balding, unsmiling, retired Army man in his seventies, the general emphasized throughout the morning conference that, although he realized conscientious objection to war does exist, he himself could not understand why Muste and his associates—including a young, attractive housewife and a soft-spoken Quaker lady—were protesting civil defense. "After all," the general mustered his patience at one point, "you're among the people we're working to protect."

General Huebner directed his aides, who were nervously and quickly deferential to his authority, to explain the civil defense law. The main event was a lecture—illustrated with slides—on how the civil defense network would function in the event of an attack. Muste, taking notes, watched intently in the darkened room. Huebner, who had seen the slides many times before, rose in relief when the lights went on.

Muste, the spokesman for the visitors, also stood. "We do appreciate this briefing," he said to the general, who began to smile. "But," Muste continued, stuffing his notes in his pocket, "our worst fears have been confirmed by this presentation. Civil defense, after all, is an integral part of the total preparations for nuclear war. We, on the other hand, are convinced that the only way to a secure defense is for people to refuse to participate in any way in the preparations for war."

The general advised Muste to petition his Congressman, and added, "You can also make your views known in other ways, You're free; you're white . . ." The general stopped.

"We would have been very pleased," Muste said quickly, "if some of the Negroes in our group could have been here this morning."

"Of course, of course," said the general who was becoming somewhat exacerbated. "In any case, we must protect ourselves. When war does come, and you people don't want to participate, we don't give a hoot if you want to sit on the street and fry. We'll bury you. And if you're hurt, we'll take care of you. Civil defense is part of our national security system. I would put you in the class of a subversive if you didn't obey the law."

After more conversation between the general and Muste, the former suggested, "Perhaps you might arrange to be indoors during the drills. That way you won't subject yourselves to regulations that require you to seek shelter."

"No," Muste answered politely. "We do not intend to avoid the drills. Millions of Americans do just that. They have no confidence in the effectiveness of civil defense and manage to be indoors when the sirens go off. In a sense, that's their form of protest. But it's not our way. We do not, for example, evade the draft. We resist it. And we shall resist the drills."

The delegation left the puzzled general. "The thing about A.J.," the Quaker lady said as Muste hurried to the subway for a committee meeting uptown, "is that he gives you a place you can put your feet down in this sort of protest. He not only works out so much of the strategy and organization, but he sets the climate. Even General Huebner could see that A.J. is no crackpot."

"It also helps," said an atheist among the pacifists, "that A.J. is a preacher. Sometimes he can get in to see people we can't. And besides, having a Reverend as a spokesman makes us appear less like a bunch of nuts."

Muste is indeed a minister, but he has been almost entirely inactive in that role since becoming a full-time peace agitator more than twenty years ago. Technically, Muste is still a Presbyterian clergyman, but he has crossed several denominational lines in his complex career. Although, for example, he also remains a member of the Society of Friends, he was first ordained in the Calvinist Dutch Reformed Church. During the First World War, however, Muste was minister of a Congregational Church in Newtonville, Massachusetts, but was forced to resign that post because of his unyielding pacifism. Many years later, Muste met a former Newtonville parishioner who told him, "You saved my soul. If you had backed down then, I wouldn't have gone on believing in God."

Nor has Muste always been primarily a pacifist. He became a labor leader in 1919; directed Brookwood

Labor College in the 1920's; and in the early 1930's, he headed a radical political party, eventually allying himself and his followers with the Trotskyites. The contentious Leon Trotsky looked on Muste as a considerable asset to his American forces, and was disappointed when Muste suddenly returned to religion and pacifism in 1936.

Since then, Muste has remained a radical politically, but has concentrated his enormous energies on turning American pacifism into a mass, direct-action movement based on the philosophy and techniques of nonviolent resistance.

Reverend Muste hasn't had a church since 1940, when he became the Executive Secretary of the Fellowship of Reconciliation, a nondenominational peace organization which is also active in civil rights, labor relations, and other areas requiring conciliatory skills. The only pastoral functions Muste has performed in the past two decades are occasional marriage ceremonies for children of old radical friends who would otherwise find it difficult to invite a man of the cloth to their homes. On those assignments, Muste usually reads a Shakespeare sonnet or selects for his text a poem by safely nondenominational contemporaries such as Stephen Spender. "I don't use the Bible," says the nondoctrinaire preacher, "unless I'm asked to bring it."

When engaged in his main line of work, direct action against war, Muste works with as little self-consciousness or strain among the most resolutely atheistic pacifists as he does with church peacemakers. The nonreligious War Resisters League presented him its Peace Award in 1958. Ralph Di Gia, Administrative Secretary of the W.R.L., notes appreciatively: "When A.J. is with us, he leaves out the God stuff, and he'll occasionally say 'hell' and 'damn.'" On the other hand, to use a recurring

Muste phrase, Muste until recently was also Chief Missioner of the Church Peace Mission, which is composed of the historic peace churches—the Brethren, the Friends, the Mennonites, the Fellowship of Reconciliation, and other similarly oriented North American fellowships. "One night," says Di Gia, "he'll be talking to the Young People's Socialist League at Debs Hall in Greenwich Village, and the next week, he'll be speaking for the Church Peace Mission, debating a nonpacifist professor of theology at a divinity school."

Among peace groups of all persuasions, secular and religious, Muste has long been recognized as a remarkably effective reconciler. Pacifists, being nonconformists, are usually extremely individualistic, and anger is not unknown in their private conclaves. Muste, however, is welcome in nearly all camps. One veteran of many acidulous, if nonviolent, skirmishes in the movement, has described a difficult five-year period in the late 1940's and early 1950's during which Muste somehow held together one particularly turbulent group, the Peacemakers: "The differences among these radical pacifists were deep and irreconcilable with respect to religion, government, the democratic process, and their own problems of organization and leadership. But while he was Secretary, A.J.'s capacity for reconciliation was so great that he was able to pull us through each annual conference without undue violence."

At a celebration of his seventieth birthday at the Community Church in New York in 1955, some five hundred guests paid Muste unstinted tribute. Present were pacifists of many varieties, labor officials, clerics of several denominations, Negro leaders, and unorganized friends. John Oliver Nelson, Professor of Christian Vocation at the Yale University Divinity School, looked at the crowd, and noted dryly, "About the only issue on which these people can agree is that they admire A.J."

In January, 1960, Sidney Lens, a nonpacifist labor leader who has been a close associate of Muste for many years, was chairman of a similarly heterogeneous celebration in Chicago of Muste's seventy-fifth birthday. Lens solemnly presented Muste on that occasion with a 25-inch pole-vaulting stick. "With this," he told the agile pacifist, "you won't have to climb those fences."

On April 21, 1960, there was another birthday tribute to Muste at the Community Church in New York. Among the scores of messages was a letter from Martin Niemoeller: "It is almost unbelievable that this year you will be 75. . . . I wish you to know that your example has been before my eyes for many years as a symbol of courage and perseverance and undaunted faithfulness." Iwao Ayusawa of the Fellowship of Reconciliation of Japan wrote from Tokyo and recalled Muste's years as a labor leader after the First World War: "You may remember the days of most active evangelism which you were conducting in the industrial areas around Paterson and Passaic, New Jersey. But of course you cannot remember a young uncouth Japanese boy mingled among the multitudes that were listening to you intensely. . . . It is the fire I caught then at those gatherings which I am trying to keep burning still, half a century after."

The wife of a man who had been a conscientious objector during the Second World War added a handwritten note to her husband's birthday letter to Muste. "Let the others sing your praises for your courage, intelligence, energy and great spiritual fortitude. I sing your praises because you were and are the kind of man who— on a Christmas Day of a busy war year—could take the time to write a word of good cheer and love to a lonely wife whose husband was in prison. It is the two sides of you put together that brings joy to the heart."

Sidney Hook, Professor of Philosophy at New York University, wrote: "Although I believe that your present course of absolute pacifism is tragically mistaken, and would ensure the death of free societies under Communist terror, I am happy to see that you are still as 'left' as ever—in the sense in which I define it. I honor you for it. Perhaps if people like you were permitted to survive under Communism, instead of being among the first who are liquidated, I might accept the risks of its brutal triumph to the risks of opposing it." Writer and longtime pacifist Milton Mayer sent a note: "Is that old pogo-stick only seventy-five? I thought he was a hundred seventy-five. I want to speak of the one thing that I know he has done that cannot be undone. He changed my life. I can imagine that he has changed many lives; though to have changed only one is to have changed the world. We know that there is no other way. May his embodied soul go racing—never marching on."

Mayer once described a Quaker Meeting in the summer of 1940 on the shore of one of the Finger Lakes in New York. The Friends were in silent worship. "A man stood up, a long stringy man about six feet high that you'd say had been disjointed and reassembled. He had a big sloping forehead wrinkled like the back of his pants knees, a big nose, big ears set at 45 degrees, a nice wide mouth, and a nice mop of brown and gray hair. You wouldn't say how old he was; he had the seasoned skin of country men; it doesn't change much.

" 'If I can't love Hitler,' he said, 'I can't love at all.'

"Then he sat down. . . . He wasn't preaching or confessing. He was saying something to himself, and his voice had picked it up and amplified it; it came from the very center of the man. He had moved to testify. I was getting the idea of Quakerism, and of A. J. Muste."

Along with Mayer's birthday message was one from Byron Johnson, then a Congressman from Colorado: "We have learned some special things from A.J. because he embarrasses us by being a challenge."

Muste himself was somewhat embarrassed by the adulatory tone of the birthday encomiums. A remarkably serene man, he is neither given to zealotry nor self-congratulation. Nearly as well oriented in baseball as in pacifism, politics, and the history of Marxism, Muste laughs a good deal more than most jousters for minority causes, and he is particularly disinclined to take himself too seriously. He roared when he was presented with the pole-vault stick at the Chicago birthday dinner, and his general taste in humor is reflected by his still vernal enhusiasm for the Marx Brothers.

Muste sometimes, in fact, appears so guileless that several nonpacifist churchmen and secular radicals agree with Reinhold Niebuhr that he is a "perfect innocent." Yet, Walter G. Muelder, Dean of the Boston University School of Theology, is convinced that Muste has made the peace movement "an aggressive and dynamic force for social change and has compelled Christian thought to accept full responsibility for the qualitative texture of social life. He did not, like many pacifists, find it possible to stand pat on traditional peace attitudes and static political answers, but has infused the peace movement with a faith that all the institutions of society can be transformed in principle to nonviolent ones. This means that he remains a radical on all social fronts and is not a single-cause pacifist."

"It was Muste," says Professor John Oliver Nelson of Yale, "who kept the peace movement in this country from becoming a clubwoman's organization. Moreover, he went further than pacifism. He's never believed that if there were no more war, man would automatically become good. He feels the heart of man requires radical redemption and his institutions must, as a result, be changed accordingly. A.J. is a devastating reminder to the young pacifists of what a real radical is."

2

THE
PHILOSOPHY

*"Those Who Undertake a Revolution
Are Obligated to Try at Least to See It
Through."*

THROUGH all the spirals of his half century of political
activity, Muste has been consistently skeptical of conventional "liberalism"—pacifist and nonpacifist. His
basic credo is that major social dislocation is necessary
to achieve a just society. Along with social dislocation
there must also be, of course, a radical change in individuals. And for any sizable, meaningful alteration of
society, to take place, there have to be many more than
the "too few, pathetically few" Muste-like revolutionaries currently available.

In his attempts to convert, therefore, Muste refuses
to soften his message. He is not searching for liberals.
He is trying to breed radicals. "We are now in an age,"
Muste wrote in the summer of 1962, "when men will
have to choose deliberately to exchange the values, the
concepts of 'security,' and much else which characterizes
contemporary society, and seek another way of life. If
that is so, then the peace movement has to act on that
assumption, and this means that the whole picture of

our condition and the radical choice must be placed before people—not a diluted gospel, a program geared to what they are ready to 'buy now.' "

By Muste's criteria of the possible, he feels that the chance for the growth of the quality of radicalism he means has been markedly expanded by what he calls the "new phase" into which pacifism has moved in recent years. "The shift of emphasis," he explains, "is toward the Gandhian, the sociopolitical expression of nonviolence, rather than toward the traditional Anglo-Saxon, more individualistic type. Put very simply, to young people today the question of what one's personal position is to be if nuclear warfare breaks out seems a very minor if not wholly academic matter. For them the question is how such a war can be prevented. We operate now in the realm of political decision. We are not as yet, save perhaps in a very limited sense, a mass movement. But we are not any longer a sectarian—using the term in a good sense—movement, existing apart from the main political decisions and affecting them only in a very long-range and indirect sense. We now function in mass movements and have an impact on them. Nonviolence applied to international relations, to national struggles for independence, and to race struggles, is a significant factor in contemporary political life."

In this country, Muste has long been active in the development of nonviolent techniques in the various campaigns for racial integration as well as those for peace. While Muste was Executive Secretary of the Fellowship of Reconciliation from 1940-53, he continually encouraged his field workers to accelerate integration. He also brought into the F.O.R. young organizers who became deeply influenced by his advocacy of nonviolent resistance as a social action technique and who applied

Muste's lesson throughout the country. Several of them were instrumental in the founding of C.O.R.E. (The Congress of Racial Equality) in 1942 while they were still on the staff of Fellowship of Reconciliation. Muste encouraged the establishment of C.O.R.E., and for the first four years of its existence, he was its chief fund raiser. The consistently successful desegregation projects of C.O.R.E. are based on relentless pressure through nonviolent resistance. Most of those who now see Muste's name in the long list which comprises C.O.R.E.'s National Advisory Committee are unaware of the key role he played in setting up its basic orientation and in finding the young men who would make the concept work.

Another Musteite in the F.O.R. was Bayard Rustin. Now with the War Resisters League as Executive Secretary, Rustin is one of the shrewdest and boldest tacticians in the campaigns for racial equality in America. Unlike his mild-mannered mentor, Rustin, a tall Negro in his early fifties with the bearing of a guerrilla leader, is a fiery speaker and can be ruthless in debate. In addition to his work for C.O.R.E. in that organization's early years, Rustin was later a close adviser to Martin Luther King. He helped organize the Montgomery bus boycott and was an important factor in the formation of King's Southern Christian Leadership Conference. Rustin also was in charge of correlating financial and scholarship aid for students involved in the sit-ins. "During all my work with Martin King," says Rustin, "I never made a difficult decision without talking the problem over with A.J. first."

Martin Luther King has invited Muste to lecture in the South on nonviolent resistance and says that his own ideas have been considerably influenced by Muste. King is a member of the Fellowship of Reconciliation.

Before he came to know and work with Muste in that
context, however, King, as a student at Crozer Theological Seminary in Pennsylvania, had heard Muste lecture.
"I wasn't a pacifist then," recalls King, "but the power
of A.J.'s sincerity and his hardheaded ability to defend
his position stayed with me through the years. Later, I
got to know him better, and I would say unequivocally
that the current emphasis on nonviolent direct action in
the race relations field is due more to A.J. than to anyone else in the country."

Muste characteristically applies a social revolutionary
approach to race relations. In May, 1960, he and Bayard Rustin prepared a long editorial, "Struggle for Integration," for *Liberation*, a small, lively monthly on
word affairs. Muste and Rustin are among the coedi-
tors. The bristling article—and corollary analyses in succeeding years—emphasized that the bus boycott and the
sit-ins were useful beginnings, but were only beginnings.

"Those who undertake a revolution," the editorial
proclaimed, "are obligated to try at least to see it
through. By definition, they have undertaken a job
which cannot be accomplished entirely, or perhaps even
mainly, through the existing social and political machinery. . . . Mass action is a mere gesture unless those
who engage in it are prepared for mass arrests. . . .
Without claiming that in all cases, accepting bail, plead-
ing not guilty and standing trial, appealing cases to
higher courts, paying fines, etc., must be rejected, these
things cannot be the central policy of a mass movement.
They eat up money, and place the movement for liberation in a defensive position. They are likely to stall mass
action until, months or years later, the outcome of
appeals is decided. It all amounts to acquiescing in the
slow grinding of the machinery which is there precisely

to prevent the changes the mass movement seeks. It is more effective to fill the jails and use the money for the families of the volunteers than to throw it into the jaws of the legal mills. The thesis that mass action leads to jail applies to leaders as well as the rank and file."

Two years later, Muste clarified his attitude toward the relative importance of serving time as a concomitant of radical mass action, whether for peace or integration. "I come out of a tradition," he noted, "which holds that you do your revolutionary job and if that lands you in jail, fine. You never compromise or 'chicken out' in order to keep out of jail. But there is no special virtue about getting into jail, *per se;* the basic orientation is not an ascetic one. The main fact, however, is that there are not enough people in jail because we are not working at our job hard enough."

The 1960 editorial in *Liberation* had gone on to explain a basic element in the philosophy of nonviolence. "Martin King exhorts his fellow Negroes to 'love your enemies,' and there is reason to think that a good many people, especially the young, misunderstand that phrase . . . it does not mean having a sentimental liking for people who spit on you." According to Muste and Rustin, the term *does* mean that for Negroes to "love" white Southerners, they must recognize both that the whites have the capacity to be "fully human," and that they cannot fulfill that capacity until the present social structure in the South is changed. The aim, therefore, of mass direct action in the South is to "remove the present social structure." Accordingly, the editorial concludes, "in carrying on their relentless nonviolent struggle for their own liberation, *Negroes are liberating white Southerners.* This is the basic way in which the former express their 'love' for the latter."

In applying the techniques of nonviolence to labor

disputes, peace demonstrations, and desegregation projects, Muste continually emphasizes that "nonviolence is
not a negative thing. It does not mean the absence of
violence, the renunciation of action, submission. It
means resort to a superior form of struggle, the tapping
of the reservoirs of moral force—'soul force,' as Gandhi
called it." Muste has often been asked whether the persistent "soul force" generated by stubborn resistance to
militarism or segregation is not itself the placing of
undue pressure, however nonviolently, on other human
beings. Muste, for instance, has advocated confrontation
of segregationists and the "military machine" with the
demonstrators' own bodies. The sit-ins were one example of this technique. Another, as in various civil
disobedience demonstrations with which Muste has
been affiliated, has involved pacifists sitting or standing
in the way of trucks on the way to a missile base, and
refusing to move.

These amiably implacable resisters are practicing
what Richard Gregg, a leading tactician of the movement, calls "moral jiujitsu." In his *The Power of Nonviolence* (Fellowship Publications), a basic work for
apprentices, Gregg explains that: "The nonviolence
and good will of the victim act in the same way that
the lack of physical opposition by the user of physical
jiujitsu does, causing the attacker to lose his moral balance. He suddenly and unexpectedly loses the moral
support which the usual violent resistance of most victims would render him. He plunges forward, as it were,
into a new world of values. He feels insecure because
of the novelty of the situation and his ignorance of how
to handle it. He loses his poise and self-confidence. The
victim not only lets the attacker come, but, as it were,
pulls him forward by kindness, generosity and voluntary
suffering, so that the attacker loses his moral balance."

Muste is convinced that "moral jiujitsu" works, and was not surprised when the Southern Regional Council released a report in November, 1960, pointing out that the Negro sit-ins had forced an unprecedented reversal of roles on Southern police. "For too many years in the South," the report said, "the police were assumed to be an arm of the white race to keep the Negroes in their place." After months of mass nonviolent resistance by Negroes, the Southern policeman "now, to maintain law and order, . . . must protect the nonviolent Negroes from the whites. And, he must do it quickly."

Although admitting the frequent effectiveness of non-violent resistance, one troubled pacifist wrote Muste several years ago about the possible moral contradictions involved in this kind of provocative direct action. The questioner wondered whether, when a pacifist pushes another person beyond the latter's "limit of toleration" and drives him to anger, the pacifist hasn't seduced his opponent into committing violence. Perhaps the pacifist has not indeed spoken to the highest in the other person but instead has "created enmity" between the two.

In his answer, Muste noted: "It has been said that people become pacifists because they have deep-seated aggressive impulses which they 'repress' but which are there nevertheless and make pacifists *want* to provoke others. It is clear, in any case, that where there is to be such confrontation as we are discussing, the utmost effort must be made to try to tell others what it is we are doing and why. This having been said, however, it must also be pointed out that the fact that men may resent non-violent action and may attack and crucify those who engage in it is not automatically proof that the spirit of nonviolence has been betrayed, that the 'highest' in the other has not been appealed to. It is all too well known that one generation reveres, perhaps deifies, those whom its predecessors crucified. There are, furthermore, many instances where those who were aroused to the greatest bitterness and violence prove to have been most deeply touched and become the most ardent converts to the cause whose adherents they persecuted. The classic example in Christian history is, of course, Paul, who was among those who were 'touched in their hearts' at the preaching of Stephen and who nevertheless 'gnashed on him with their teeth.' "

Muste ended by emphasizing that "reconciliation is not synonymous with smoothing things over in the conventional sense. Reconciliation, in every relationship, requires bringing the deep causes of conflict to the surface and that may be very painful. It is when the deep differences have been faced and the pain of that experienced, that healing and reconciliation may take place."

As the *Liberation* editorial and the reply to the disturbed pacifist indicate, Muste is continually suspicious of exactly how such terms as "love" and "reconciliation" are used. "You have to get back of words," he has often told visitors to his small, cluttered, one-room-with-kitchen-alcove in the Masters Apartments on the upper West Side of Manhattan. On one such occasion toward the end of 1962, Muste stopped his correspondence to elaborate on the point for an apprentice "nuclear pacifist." It was ten in the morning, and, as is his custom, Muste had already been at work for more than an hour. Manuscripts, books and newspapers were all over the room—in cases, on tables, and on his bed.

"So often the preachers of love," Muste stopped to light a cigarette, "rebuke people for not loving enough, without realizing that the way they themselves wave the word around is an assertion that they're superior and are entitled to make moral judgments on others. Many of those preachers are actually expressing rejection when they speak of 'love.' That's why, although I often disagree with Reinhold Niebuhr, I do believe there is an element of truth in the reemphasis on the sinful corruption of human beings that has been made by Niebuhr and the other neo-orthodox theologians. Where Niebuhr's judgment is, I think, defective, is that he doesn't take account of all the aspects of St. Paul's spiritual paradox, 'Where sin abounds, grace much more abounds.' Niebuhr cautions us to be constantly aware of the obverse, 'Where grace abounds, sin still exists,' so that when you think you're being very loving, you may well be hating in subtle ways. Yet, as Erich Fromm and others have indicated, when you do become aware of the aggression and hate in yourself, it's then that you become capable of loving. I am more hopeful than Niebuhr that we can achieve a social revolution through changing human beings as well as their institutions by making them aware of both the sin and the grace they contain. But I agree with Niebuhr that simply advocating 'love' won't do it.

"I was not impressed with the sentimental, easygoing pacifism of the earlier part of the century. People then felt that if they sat and talked pleasantly of peace and love, they would solve the problems of the world. Norman Vincent Peale, for another example, is someone for whom it is very difficult for me to have respect. I don't question his subjective sincerity, but, on the other hand, he has no conception, it seems to me, of the tragic aspects of life and the possibilities of evil in all of us. Nor does he seem aware of the social implications of the Gospel. As a result, he can go on Sunday after Sunday, preaching 'Have faith in yourself, think cheerfully, and the world will be cheerful.' This is simply an incantation of the superficial. Besides, Peale hobnobs with the big boys all the time. That's no place for a Christian preacher."

Muste, except for occasional fund-raising visits to the rich, does not "hobnob with the big boys." He has no bank account; his income is small; and, for long periods of time, he gives the impression of owning only one suit. During one birthday party in his honor in 1950, a fund was raised for him, but the check was pointedly given to the late Mrs. Muste. "Otherwise," Muste was told at the dinner, "you'd use it for a cause." Mrs. Muste thanked the donors for their concern, kept $500 of the fund, and gave the other $2,000 to the Fellowship of Reconciliation.

A veteran of the union battles of thirty and forty years ago has told Milton Mayer of having attended a large strike meeting in Paterson, New Jersey, in 1931: "I was down and out, on strike, and my shoes were so thin I could feel the cold through the soles. All the do-gooders were on the platform to pep us up and raise the relief fund. I was in the first row of the audience, and right up above me, on the platform, was this long skinny fellow. I never saw such long legs on a man, and he kept crossing them to get them out of the way, but pretty soon they'd start swinging, and I saw the bottom of each of his shoes; the soles were gone and he had newspapers in them. I turned to the fellow next to me and asked him who it was. He said, 'It's Muste. Used to be a preacher before he went straight.' "

3

THE
CALVINIST
YEARS

*"There Is No Telling What Goes into the
Education of a Pacifist."*

ALTHOUGH his shoes have usually had soles, A. J. Muste
has never known a surfeit of material goods. He was
born in the small town of Zierikzee in the province of
Zeeland in the Netherlands on January 8, 1885. His
parents, Martin Muste and Adriana Jonker, named
their first boy Abraham Johannes. (His relatives later
came to call him "Bram" or "Brammie," but, for over
fifty years, everyone else with whom he is in contact for
any length of time invariably comes to refer to him as
"A.J.")

"My mother," Muste recalled during a series of
rambling autobiographical sketches for *Liberation*, "re-
marked that during the first year of my existence I cried
virtually without interruption all day but slept like
a top all night. This was a pattern which I have in some
sense followed most of my life, since I am usually sound-
ing off about something a good part of every day and
practically never have any trouble sleeping at night."

As coachman to a family of the provincial nobility,

Martin Muste's future in the Netherlands was limited, particularly since the economy as a whole was not especially fluid, with few facilities for industrial expansion. Four of his wife's brothers, who had been poorly paid agricultural workers in Zeeland, had already emigrated to America. On a trip home, one of the brothers convinced the Mustes to follow them. The brothers also volunteered to finance the trip.

Muste's uncles had gone into small business—groceries, drugs, scrap metal—in Grand Rapids, Michigan, where thousands of Hollanders had settled since the middle of the nineteenth century. "The emigrants from the Netherlands," Muste points out, "didn't often try farming when they came here, because most of the available jobs by that time were in the rapidly developing industries. Some stayed in New York and New Jersey, where the Dutch had settled in colonial days; but most followed the territory that was being developed along the Erie Canal and the New York Central Railroad tracks. Cities like Grand Rapids, for example, were expanding swiftly. When my family arrived in 1891, the population was some 50,000. By the time I was twenty, it had doubled."

The Muste family traveled to America in steerage through two stormy weeks in January, 1891. "Families staked out preserves for themselves on the platforms, one above the other, which served as beds. Those who were near the wall, as we were, climbed over the families between them and the aisle when occasion arose. Occasionally soup was passed out, but the migrants had brought their own supplies of bread and cheese with them, and in some instances cakes, which they occasionally shared with families like ours who had none. It was all new experience; it was adventure; and it was to my liking."

Adriana Muste became ill during the voyage, and, when the ship docked, she was hospitalized for a month on Ellis Island. Her son couldn't understand English, but became intrigued when an attendant, having discovered the boy's first name, kept calling him "Abraham Lincoln." Muste recalls that he didn't know "whether Abraham Lincoln was the name of a gadget, a town, or a person dead or alive." As soon as he learned English, the boy read all he could find about Lincoln and was strongly influenced by the image he formed of the man. "In time I learned, of course, about certain distinctions between Lincoln the myth and Lincoln the human being, between the 'American dream' and the reality. Nevertheless, being called 'Abraham Lincoln' on the island in New York harbor, passing my youth in Michigan, not far from Springfield, in the 1890's when the Middle West in its own imagination and feeling still lived in the days of John Brown, the Emancipation Proclamation, the martyred President—all this is part of my inmost being."

Two days after reaching Grand Rapids, Martin Muste was hired as a teamster at six dollars a week for a sixty-hour week. "In the larger population in Grand Rapids," Muste has noted, "the Dutch constituted a lower stratum. The owners of the furniture factories and sawmills were of English stock. Until after the First World War, Hollanders were the cheap labor of the factories, the small shopkeepers in the outlying parts of town, and the poor farmers on the land. In my early youth, it was still an event when a girl from one of the Dutch families, a girl who may well have been born in the United States, became a clerk in one of the fashionable department stores downtown. The girl's family, for its part, wondered whether it would not have been better if she had remained in domestic service instead of being exposed to all the lures of life in the English-speaking stratum of the town. Had not their Calvinist God assigned them their place as hewers of wood, though often highly skilled ones, and would it not be best for the children to remain close to the fold of the humble elect?" From the viewpoint, however, of the descendants of the British, "the Dutch were considered especially desirable immigrants. Almost without exception they were sober and industrious. Many of them became skilful cabinet makers. And they were allergic to unions or 'agitators' of any kind."

The Mustes attended the local Reformed Church, where the services were in Dutch. It was a stern religion. The preachers taught predestination, but, as Muste indicates, "the belief that you couldn't save yourself but were *elected* to salvation did not lead to passivity in *this* life. Although the doctrine produced some rigidly self-righteous souls convinced of their election, it also led others to social action on the Calvinistic basis that the reign of God must also be established in all areas of life on earth. In the previous history of the Dutch Reformed Church, many of its communicants developed a strong social consciousness which led them to anti-royalist political action. But the revolutionary *élan* of that application of Calvinism was almost nonexistent in the Middle Western Dutch Reformed Church in which I was raised. Its members were all Republicans and would no more have voted for a Democrat than have turned horse thief. Many who had originally come from the Netherlands had had a very difficult time there, and appreciated the larger opportunities for themselves and their children in America. They were good workmen but they were docile. They didn't want to upset the apple cart."

Martin Muste was naturalized in time to vote for

William McKinley in 1896. In the process, Abraham Muste, then eleven, became a citizen. He himself was eventually to receive occasional write-in votes for President. "I still do run into people who say they've voted for me as a radical peace candidate," Muste says. "There was one particularly insistent lady in North Carolina who habitually wrote my name in during the 1940's. I wrote her once that even if I were elected, I couldn't serve because I'd been born abroad. She wrote back angrily that I had chosen a very picayune, jingoistic excuse."

The Muste household in Grand Rapids was conservative in politics, and orthodox in religion. "But," says Muste, "there was not a pervasive sense of imminent hellfire. None of us children was exposed to the constant terror of being nonelected and, therefore, eternally damned that a number of our contemporaries experienced. Both our parents, especially my mother, were strict and we were occasionally spanked, but discipline was more by moral than physical pressure. We were strongly indoctrinated with the conviction that we must never do anything to shame the family and never put on airs. For example, when I was seventeen and attending Hope College in Holland, Michigan, I won the state oratorical contest, the first time that anyone from that little Dutch school had triumphed in the competition. I returned to the college from the contest on the last day of the term. Classes had been suspended." Muste was met at the depot with a carriage decorated in orange and black. He was drawn through the principal streets of the town, accompanied by students blowing horns, waving brooms, and shouting the Hope College yell. In the procession were fifty girls tramping through the mud after their champion. "As a result of the celebration," Muste recalls, "I was late getting home, and my mother was angry. She made no fuss over my having won. She was proud, but she didn't want me to feel I was a big shot. She reminded me instead that I'd failed in my duty to be on time."

No dancing was allowed among the Dutch emigrants in Grand Rapids. "It was also sinful to sing popular tunes," Muste remembers, "and we were restricted to hymns and to beautifully translated metrical versions of the Book of Psalms that are far superior to the doggerel of the Scotch and English translations." The theater and dance—for which Muste has since developed a considerable affection—were also proscribed. Smoking was not. "We came from the Continent, where Calvinist customs were somewhat more liberal than in England and Scotland." During the first couple of years after the Mustes' arrival, the parents continued drinking beer, as they had in the Netherlands, but they gradually stopped, since orthodox Protestants in the Midwest at the time regarded drinking as sinful.

"In spite of the surface Puritanism and the strict rules," Muste emphasizes, "we were a close, loving family. My relationship with my parents even survived my radicalism. When I had to leave my church during the First World War, the break was hard for my parents to accept, but they also understood that my refusal to support war was hardly unchristian. In later years, although they didn't always agree with what I was doing, they did feel that I should act according to my beliefs. My father, who outlived my mother, finally came to agree with my pacifism. He also finally questioned at least a few of the defects in the economy toward the end of his life. He was angry when he was laid off during the Depression. In his mid-seventies, still vigorous, my father had done hard manual work all his life and he couldn't understand why there wasn't a place for him." Adriana Muste was slight and short but was a strong, active woman. "She did reflect the tensions of having had to bring up five children during years when she occasionally also had to take in washing. But when she passed fifty-five, she relaxed and had an exceptionally jolly life until she died at eighty-three." Her husband lived to be eighty-seven.

Of the Muste children, three sisters, two married and one a widow, still live in Grand Rapids. A younger brother, Cornelius Muste, now retired, served for many years as a pastor in Brooklyn and in Medford Lakes, New Jersey. Cornelius Muste recalls that "we first went to a Dutch parochial school in Grand Rapids, but we were soon transferred to the public school. We hadn't known a word of English when we came, but by the time A.J. had finished the eighth grade, he'd won a prize of $15 for the best essay in his class on the subject of child labor. The prize money, contributed by the Trades and Labor Council of Grand Rapids, was to be used on books, an enthusiasm of A.J. In fact, I can't remember a time when he didn't have a book in his hand."

Muste had to accept the recommendations of a representative of the Trades and Labor Council when the time came to buy the books. He somewhat dourly took home *Self Help* by Samuel Smiles, a standard self-improvement guide which lectured the young on the economic as well as moral advantages of frugality, sobriety, and industriousness. "I have never been drunk," Muste reflected sixty years later, "and I am, I suppose, industrious—but from preference, not from a sense of duty. My tastes are simple, but I have a considerable aversion to saving and a strong aversion to moneymaking."

Muste was much more interested in several of the other prize books, particularly an Agnes Repplier poetry anthology, which stimulated a fondness for poetry that Muste retains, and J. B. Green's *Short History of England*. The latter introduced the boy to the pleasures of history which delighted him so much that for a time in his youth he was considering abandoning the ministry and becoming a history professor. The last major prize was a collection of Emerson's *Essays*. Muste is convinced that Emerson was the most seminal influence on his thinking at the time because of his emphasis on personal responsibility, and because "he conveyed the spirit of American life as I was experiencing it as a boy in Michigan. His essays actually were a song of praise to the American dream as it seemed then."

Muste found school a source of infinite pleasure. "It was an utter fascination. That apparently there would never be an end of things to learn frequently produced a state of delightful intoxication. I learned that when I had graduated from the eighth grade, there would be awesome subjects ahead, like algebra, physiology, geology, psychology, not to mention the ultimate wonderlands of theology, predestination, apologetics, eschatology. The words themselves were blessed."

The boy also became insatiably interested in the Civil War, having come upon bound volumes of *Harper's* and *Century*. He tried to interview veterans in the Old Soldiers' Home in town. "When I did, I was usually grumpily rebuffed, and this was hard to understand. Why shouldn't they be eager to speak of the glorious battles they had fought? Occasionally, one of them did talk. 'Yes, I lost a leg at Chickamauga,' and spun a tale. What a day that was!" Muste kept seeing the old soldiers making a regular trip downtown every day after lunch. "It was to be quite a few years before I knew that what my heroes went downtown for was booze, and that veterans of wars are not always, not nearly always, heroic noblemen who volunteered to lay down their lives so that some great cause might not perish from the earth. The moral of all this may be that there is no telling what goes into the education of a pacifist."

His brothers and sisters remember that Muste was somewhat of a religious mystic from the time he was quite young. When he was in his early seventies, Muste could still picture clearly the Sundays he spent in the Dutch Reformed Church in Grand Rapids: "The preacher in his Prince Albert walked to the pulpit; the old organ played as softly as it could. Then the service began. I must have been no older than six or seven when all this gave me a feeling of having entered another world, the 'real' world, the feeling, which later I found conveyed in one of the New Testament Epistles, that one had come 'to Mount Zion, the city of the living God, the heavenly Jerusalem, to myriads of angels in festal gathering, to the assembly of the first-born enrolled in heaven, to God the judge of all, to the spirits of just men made perfect.' "

On weekdays, there were distinctly corporeal forces with which the boy had to deal. When Muste was eleven and in the seventh grade, he deliberately tripped the class bully one morning as the latter came through the aisle toward the teacher's desk for a routine chastisement. An after-school battle was inevitable. Circled by their expectant classmates, Muste and the older, bigger boy confronted each other. "For some unfathomable reason I no longer felt afraid or nervous, as I had up to that moment. He said belligerently, 'You tripped me.' I looked him in the eye and allowed as how I had. He probably felt I would try to lie my way out of the situation, or put up my fists and make the best fight I could. When I did neither, he was taken off guard. He hesitated, shifted his weight to the other leg, hitched one of his shoulders, turned and walked away without saying a word. His pals followed him. In a moment, the other boys, considerably disappointed, walked off."

The incident made sufficient impression on Muste so that he frequently relived the scene for years afterward. Decades later, Muste finally concluded that the encounter had involved several elements of the philosophy of pacifism that he had not consciously adopted until 1915. "In the first place," he has explained, talking of himself as an eleven-year-old in the third person, "the boy did the unexpected. The conventional action in such a situation is fight or flight. And the opponent knows by habit or instinct how to respond.

"When he meets an unexpected reaction, it's as if 'moral jiujitsu' has been performed on him. In any pacifism which is not cowardice or at best mere passivity, there must be this factor of spontaneity and imagination. One of the chief marks of our fallen condition is that in a world where no two human beings are exactly alike, we usually behave like figures in a drill. Well did Auden pray, 'Prohibit sharply the rehearsed response.'

"Secondly," Muste further explores the day nonviolence was applied in Grand Rapids, "the boy told the truth. This is also a very revolutionary thing to do. I'm not making any claims about knowing 'the truth' or being immune from self-deceit. I'm speaking only of a disposition to tell the truth as one sees it in a situation of tension and conflict. It's unusual even in face-to-face relationships and is not expected at all between nations. Yet everyone has experienced what a cleanliness and a healing come into a situation when nobody is trying to hide anything any more. I'm thinking of what many Southerners will say about race only for private consumption; or nuclear scientists about war.

"Third, the boy admitted he was in the wrong. When the battle was impending, he said he had done the deed. This isn't often done, even in good society. And who ever expects a nation to admit that it's in the wrong? Fourth, the boy was not afraid. Someone afraid, under tension, creates tension in others, makes *them* afraid. Finally, the boy, having, as it were, made himself defenseless, found himself safe. I'm convinced from experience that spiritual forces are as real as physical power. The trouble mainly is that we want to have both. We want to trust in God and have plenty of H-bombs too, just in case. But we can't have it both ways. We have to choose on what level, and with what weapons, we'll wage the battle, and accept the risks and consequences involved. There are risks either way."

Having begun to learn more than the books in grammar school taught him, Muste left home in September, 1898, to attend the preparatory school of Hope College, a Dutch Reformed school in Holland, Michigan, twenty-five miles away. Several months before, he had been accepted into membership in the Fourth Reformed Church of Grand Rapids at the unusually early age of thirteen. Soon after, his application to study for the ministry was approved and he was allotted the small sum of money that made it possible for him to attend the preparatory school. To earn extra cash, Muste worked in the library at Hope. "This gave me access to books on evolution which were kept locked from younger students and were issued only to college upperclassmen, under strict supervision. I remember being scolded by a seminarian from my home church in Grand Rapids for tasting, surreptitiously, of the forbidden fruit. He threatened to tell my parents, which caused me some apprehension but did not stop me from slipping into the stacks. However, he did not carry out this threat. He also predicted that 'all this will come to no good end,' and here, of course, he was right."

While at Hope, "Abe" (as he was known to his classmates) also worked in the dining hall, was captain of the state championship basketball team, played second base on the baseball team, and was valedictorian. His oratorical victories also continued. One prize-winning speech, "The Problem of Discontent," began: "The inevitable fruit of all life and progress is dissatisfaction and unrest." The climax of the oration came when the twenty-year-old proclaimed: "The eternal unrest of humanity and the discontent of the soul urge men to action, and in action is the principle of all progress on the part of the race and the ultimate warrant of peace to the individual." Thirty years later, a nephew sent Muste a copy of the speech. "I was astonished," Muste says, "at what it foretold of my life."

Muste was graduated from Hope College at twenty. He spent the next year teaching Greek and Latin in Orange City, Iowa, "to the sons and daughters of devout Iowa corn growers." There was, however, a more primary reason for Muste's postponing further graduate work in the East than an overwhelming desire to educate agrarians. At the start of his senior year at Hope, Muste had fallen in love instantly with Anna Huizenga, who had been raised in remote Rock Valley in the extreme northwest corner of Iowa. Her father was a minister of the Dutch Reformed Church. "Apart from whatever chemistry leads to mutual attraction," Muste reminisced fifty-five years later, "she was very fun-loving and venturesome. About three months after she'd come to the school, it was accepted that we were in love. During my year of teaching at Northwestern Classical Academy in Orange City, I was only about twenty miles from Rock Valley."

Muste and his fiancée were separated for two years when he came East in September, 1906, to enter the Theological Seminary of the Dutch Reformed Church in New Brunswick, New Jersey. "It was tough being away from her that long, but in those days, you weren't expected to get married until you had finished your training and were able to support your wife." On June 21, 1909, A. J. Muste and Anna Huizenga were married at the bride's home in Rock Valley.

4

THE FIRST
CONVERSION
TO PACIFISM

"I Could Not Adequately Comfort Them."

WHILE AT New Brunswick, a stronghold of Calvinism, Muste also took courses in philosophy at New York University and Columbia. At the latter school he heard William James lecture on pragmatism and he first met John Dewey who was to become a close friend and a supporter of Muste's administration at Brookwood Labor College in the 1920's. Muste was growing increasingly restive under the dogma of the Dutch Reformed Church, and his New York courses intensified his discontent. In 1909, after being graduated from the seminary, Muste was licensed and ordained to the ministry of the Reformed Church in America. He was appointed the first minister of the Fort Washington Collegiate Church, on Washington Heights. "One advantage of the location," Muste recalls, "was that it was only a few blocks north of where the New York Yankee ball park was then located." Another was that the liberal Union Theological Seminary was nearby. Muste took additional courses there and received a Bachelor of Divinity

degree *magna cum laude* in 1913. He found the philosophy professors at Union markedly more stimulating
than those under whom he had studied in Michigan
and New Brunswick. A major influence was Arthur
Cushman McGiffert, Sr., "whose lectures on the history
of Christian dogma were far and away the most brilliant
I have ever experienced. They eventually forced me to
an 'agonizing re-appraisal' of the beliefs on which I had
been reared." It was at a graduate seminar at Union
Theological Seminary that Muste first met Norman
Thomas, then a Presbyterian minister.

The years in New York before the First World War
also affected Muste politically. "The Republicanism in
which I had been brought up received rude shocks.
These were the years of mushrooming sweatshops, of
the terrible Triangle fire in a garment factory, of the
strikes which marked the founding of the garment trades
unions, and of the turbulent I.W.W. organizational
campaigns and strikes in Paterson and more distant
places."

In the summer of 1908, before his last year at New
Brunswick, Muste was a supply preacher at the Middle
Collegiate Church on Second Avenue and Seventh
Street, on the East Side of New York City. "For the first
time in my life I had really seen, and lived in, slums. I
had walked the streets and parks on hot summer days
and during the only slightly less oppressive evenings.
I had climbed flights of stairs to call on sick and aged
parishioners. Sometimes I had barely been able to endure the fetid smells and unceasing, raucous noises.
This was a very different poverty than that of the furni-
ture-factory workers or even that of the poor farmers of
the Middle West during 'the hard times.' " Muste began to read radical writers, and in 1912, he voted for
Socialist Eugene V. Debs. Since then, he has never voted

for a Democrat or Republican for a major national or
state office, and has, in fact, come to regard the Socialist
Party itself as insufficiently radical.

By the end of 1914, Muste felt compelled to give up
his Fort Washington ministry. He could no longer accept the entire body of Calvinist dogma nor could he
believe in the literal inspiration of the Bible. Abraham
and Anna Muste moved to Newtonville, a suburb of
Boston, where he became minister of Central Congregational Church. Their first child, Nancy, was born in
Newtonville in January, 1916.

Muste enjoyed his Massachusetts pastorate. His congregation consisted mainly of professional people who
provided him with a continuing intellectual challenge.
He was, furthermore, quickly accepted into the upper
echelon of Boston preachers and theologians. The coming of the war, however, ended his idyll. "As late as the
fall of 1914, war had not been a personal problem for
me. At that time, the Spanish-American War Veterans
Post of Washington Heights had held its annual memorial service in Fort Washington Church and I had
been asked to preach the sermon. I had made the expected, conventional observations that war is a terrible
and wicked thing and that we Americans are against
war, but that when the strong attack the weak, and
democracy and religion are in danger, then, of course,
as good Christians, we must go bravely, though reluctantly, into battle. I have often reflected since that it
would have been difficult to find a more inappropriate
event to which to relate such remarks than the Spanish-
American War. Certainly, in all the study of Scripture
through which I had been led in that citadel of orthodoxy, New Brunswick, and in the hotbed of heresy
which was Union Theological Seminary—in those days
—I had never been given an inkling that there might

be such a thing as a pacifist interpretation of the Gospel."

A year after he had moved to Newtonville, Muste was a confirmed pacifist. For months, a relentless inner debate had been going on concerning the possibility of such a phenomenon as a "just" war. He wondered increasingly whether it was ever possible to adjust the teachings of the Bible to pragmatic outer circumstances or whether the way instead, especially for a preacher, was to make "recalcitrant reality conform to the high ethical demand" of Scripture. In later years, the neo-orthodox Protestant theologians have claimed, as Reinhold Niebuhr has said in discussing Muste's pacifism, "that in any balance of power situation, whether it involves nations or capital and labor, you're always dealing with proximate values. These real problems, moreover, involve *discriminate* judgments. By contrast, the religious idealists proclaim the necessity of absolute judgments. Yet absolute idealism has little relevance to that part of everyday existence that involves self-seeking, power-bent men. Christianity is not simply the Sermon on the Mount strictly applied."

Muste's answer is: "I had received too solid a dose of Calvinism not to have a strong conviction about human frailty and corruption. But this does not alter the nature of the demand the Gospel places upon us—or, if you prefer, the demand that is placed upon us because we belong to the family of man—that we be honest and pure and that we love all men. Certainly the temptation to pride and self-righteousness is real and pervasive. But the temptation to adapt the Gospel's demand to circumstances and to abandon the hard effort to mold one's own life and the world according to that imperious demand is no less subtle and pervasive."

"I told Muste in 1936," says Niebuhr, "after he had

been a pacifist, then a revolutionary, and a pacifist once
again, that he had traveled the circle and hadn't learned
anything on the journey." Ever since, Niebuhr and
Muste have been contrasting symbols of nonpacifist and
pacifist Christianity among many churchmen, seminary
students, and lay Protestants.

In 1915, Muste had begun to move inexorably toward
pacifism. He was further influenced by reading the
Christian mystics, particularly the books on several of
them by Rufus Jones, a leading Quaker. "Thus I came
to know about Quakers of past and present, Quaker
Meetings, the Quaker 'peace testimony.' It was the first
time that these things suggested anything to me other
than the man on the Quaker Oats box."

The climate for pacifists during the First World War
became increasingly uncomfortable. "And not only for
pacifists," recalls Muste. "People began to act as ama-
teur spies and loyalty agents, reporting mysterious circles of light in the windows of neighbors living somewhere near the shore, which were assumed to be signals
to prowling submarines. Those who did not buy Liberty
(sic) bonds to finance the war were suspected, and in not
a few Middle Western areas where there were large
German settlements, they were tarred and feathered. As
one brought up to think of the Middle West as the
liberal democratic part of the land, in contrast to the
aristocratic and effete East, this shocked me. A pacifist
and nonconformist felt, and actually was, safer in the
East during World War I. Conscription meanwhile was
introduced in the land to which many had fled to escape
conscription. At the outset there was no provision whatsoever for conscientious objectors and many of them,
after being forcibly inducted into the Army, were
cruelly tortured in barracks and military prisons."

As for pacifist clergymen, the majority of Americans

agreed with Theodore Roosevelt that "the clergyman who does not put the flag above the church had better close his church, and keep it closed." In their book, *Opponents of War: 1917-1918* (University of Wisconsin Press), H. C. Peterson and Gilbert Fite wrote that "in some cases ministerial opponents of war were handled roughly, or even jailed. Reverend Samuel Siebert of Carmel, Illinois, was jailed in December, 1917, because he said in a sermon that he opposed war. In Aubudon, Iowa, two men, one of them a minister, were seized by a crowd who put ropes around their necks and dragged them toward the public square. After one of them signed a check for a thousand-dollar Liberty bond he was released. The minister was released because of the intervention of his wife. The *Sacramento Bee,* December 27, 1917, headlined the report, 'Near Lynchings Give Pro-Germans Needed Lesson.' "

During the first eight months of 1916, Muste's congregation in Newtonville appeared to accept his pacifist stand. "Towards the end of the summer, as United States entry loomed more directly," Muste has written in his sketches for an autobiography, "some warnings came of trouble ahead. The authorities of a fashionable boys' school located near the church thought it advisable not to expose the boys to pacifist corruption and decided to take them to another church on Sunday morning. . . . About the same time, a small number of the wealthier families in the church ceased attending. As these things became known in the congregation, the tradespeople and less opulent families generally began to go out of their way to show their sympathy. . . . But when the United States formally entered the War in April, 1917, the situation changed abruptly. I returned from the great anti-war demonstration in Washington . . . to lead a union Lenten service in my own church.

The young Swedenborgian minister refused to participate in the union service, even though it was in no
sense a political or anti-war service."

After a two-month vacation in the summer of 1917,
Muste realized that he would have to leave Newtonville.
"It was a psychological factor having to do with the
pastoral and counselling relationship which was decisive. This did not involve the young men who enlisted
or were drafted, with whom I had played baseball as
well as discussed Christian ethics. So far as I know,
every one of them as he left said in effect that he did
not know for sure whether I was right or wrong. He
himself 'had to go'; but he hoped I would stick to my
'pacifist guns.' It was when some of these boys were
wounded and one of them . . . was killed, that the parents and their friends felt that, holding the views I did,
I could not adequately comfort them. To tell the truth,
I did not feel that I could either. . . . I resigned."

The tension had been particularly hard on Anna
Muste, who had expected a quieter life as a minister's
wife. "All through the years," Muste says, "she stood by
me, and there were harder times after Newtonville
when we were on the edge of having nothing to live on.
She was not particularly an intellectual, but she was
interested in my ideas. I would usually read her my
articles and speeches and pay attention to her sugges-
tions. She wasn't much of a joiner, nor did she always
go along entirely with my positions.

"I think," Muste continues, "that the most difficult
time for her was in Newtonville. It was the first crisis
of that kind in our lives. The boy who had been killed
was the son of our closest neighbor. His mother was not
able to regard me as anything but a traitor after his
death, and she asked that I not come to the funeral.
Others stopped speaking to us on the street. There were

telephone callers, some of whom suggested I be strung up on a pole. I'd ask them to come over and talk about it with me, but none ever did. Anna never complained, but it could not have been pleasant for her."

For a time after leaving his church in December, 1917, Muste did volunteer work in Boston for the newly formed American Civil Liberties Union; helped improve local and national conditions for conscientious objectors; and assisted in the trials of several New England pacifists who had disobeyed various conscription laws. The Mustes finally went to Providence where he was enrolled as a minister in the Society of Friends. In return for pastoral work and some speaking, Muste was provided a home and expenses. In the basement of the old Meeting House in Providence "was a large room in which all the progressive and radical magazines and pamphlets of the day were available. On Saturday evenings throughout the war the various unorthodox, persecuted individuals in the city gathered to talk. . . . To the authorities this was a source of great concern and irritation. No attempt was ever made, however, to close the library. I am certain that the chief reason for this was that it was sponsored by the leading Friend of Providence Meeting, Charles Sisson. He had been a successful textile manufacturer, and by the time I got to know him he had retired from business and was devoting his time and money, as is frequently the case with Friends, to work for various causes, not least among them peace. He was a quiet man. I cannot believe that he ever in all his adult life raised his voice. But he had clear and strong opinions, and unlike some Quakers, held unequivocally to 'the peace testimony' against participation in war. Everybody knew that he could not be swerved by a hairsbreadth from his convictions and that his quiet voice could not be silenced.

Such was the respect and awe in which he was held in the locality that nothing with which Charles Sisson associated himself could, even in that hysterical time and war-mad city, be molested. This was one of the most beautiful and powerful exhibitions of what Gandhi called 'soul force' that I have ever seen."

Mrs. Muste was still adjusting to the upheavals in her life. One night in Providence, as the Mustes were lying in bed, talking, Anna Muste turned to her husband and said, "Please, just keep telling me about these things in which you believe, and why you believe them." Muste tells the story to indicate "how much she always wanted to understand. Experiencing that kind of communication for so many years, we were drawn much closer together, I'm sure, than if we had continued to lead a regular, predictable preacher's existence."

5

THE
LAWRENCE
STRIKE

*"What We Must Do Is Smile As We Pass
the Machine Guns and the Police."*

THE NEXT change in the Mustes' lives was to be more
drastic. In the fall of 1918, Muste, though still connected with the Providence Society of Friends, had
moved to Boston and an inexpensive house near the
Back Bay. The Muste family shared the house with
Harold Rotzel, a pacifist minister who had been forced
to resign from his church near Worcester. Muste, Rotzel, and other pacifists formed the Comradeship, for
which the house was headquarters. The main floor was
used for pacifist meetings and for radical political
groups who were not welcome anywhere else. The
young members of the Comradeship were trying to explore ways in which they could most effectively organize
their lives "in the way of truth, nonviolence and love."

Their meditations were interrupted by reports that
a large-scale strike was about to break out in the Lawrence, Massachusetts, textile mills. A huge and bitter
general strike there in 1912, led by the I.W.W., had received international attention but had not succeeded.

With hostilities about to resume, the members of he Comradeship thought the Lawrence situation might serve as a pragmatic testing ground for their conviction that nonviolent techniques could be made to work in specific social struggles. Muste and other members of the group began to visit Lawrence.

The local Quakers, along with the majority of the conservative Lawrence middle class, were convinced that a strike would lead to the arrival of the Bolshevik Revolution in Massachusetts. The owners of the textile mills were pleased at the interest Muste and his pacifist colleagues were taking in their labor troubles. Certainly, they believed, pacifists would counsel the workers against the strike. When Muste made clear that he conceived of nonviolence as a means of resistance, not submission, the Comradeship was no longer welcome in the executive offices of the Lawrence mills.

The average wage in the mills was $11 for a 54-hour week. Unemployment was rising, and the owners proposed to cut the work week, and proportionately, the wages. The workers, however, were demanding "54-48" —54 hours' pay for a 48-hour week. Muste and the other pacifist observers thought the demand reasonable, and prepared a leaflet explaining the economic facts and also detailing the appalling local housing conditions for the mill employees as well as the war profiteering on the part of some of the millowners. The unions in town were craft locals of the American Federation of Labor, which was opposed to the strike. "The men in these locals," Muste explains, "were of English, Scotch, and in a few cases, Irish descent, and they had no contact with or interest in the great mass of foreign-born workers."

What the rebellious workers mostly lacked was leadership. Few spoke English well, and many didn't speak the language at all. Furthermore, Muste recalls, "they had almost no contacts outside the mills and their respective language groups, nor did they have experience or training in organization techniques or publicity." Muste and two other ministers were by now making regular trips to Lawrence. They assured workers' meetings that they supported the strike and would help raise relief money.

On the first Monday in February, 1919, the workers left their jobs. Muste and his associates began raising relief funds in Boston. The picketing soon became bloody as police clubbed the workers with zest. The strikers' need of a leader was increasingly urgent. By the end of the first week, A. J. Muste was asked to become executive secretary of the strike committee.

Muste had not envisioned himself as a labor leader when he began visiting Lawrence, but he felt that morally he had to accept the position. Muste was suddenly in charge of 30,000 strikers representing more than twenty nationalities. Police brutality grew more abandoned, and the strikers' morale was weakening. Muste decided that he and Cedric Long, a Congregationalist minister who was part of the Comradeship, would have to lead a picket line in the hope that the police might be somewhat reluctant to batter down two ministers.

At first, Muste's strategy seemed to work. He and Long marched unscathed at the head of the picket line, but as soon as the two ministers turned off the main street, several mounted policemen cut Muste and Long off from the rest of the pickets—and the view of the crowd—and began beating them. Long immediately lost consciousness.

"They beat me around the body and legs with their clubs," Muste recalls, "taking care not to knock me unconscious, and forced me to keep walking slowly in order to avoid being trampled by the horses. We were passing a barn that seemed to be shut tight, but suddenly a door opened, an arm shot out, grabbed mine, pulled me into the shed, and slammed the door shut again. In the half-light I saw that it was a woman. She could not speak English. She hurried me to a side door of the barn, while the police clamored and cursed outside. She tried to hurry me from the barn into her house, which adjoined it. The police were too quick for her. Some of them had leaped into the yard. They grabbed me as she tried, in vain, to hang on. She let go and cursed them in their turn. The cops got me back on the sidewalk and resumed the systematic beating, with the result that before long I was too exhausted to keep on my feet and was deposited in the wagon by the side of Cedric."

For the first time, Muste was in jail. A police captain from Newton, the father of a boy who had been in Muste's Bible class there, had been loaned to the Lawrence security forces. He stopped outside Muste's cell, and made loudly clear how disgusted he was that a man of the church had so misbehaved that he had had to be jailed. A week later, the case against Muste and Long was dismissed since testimony made it evident that the peace had been disturbed by the police. The judge nonetheless sternly warned the ministers not to be caught again on a picket line.

The strike continued. Over a hundred strikers were arrested, and the police finally placed machine guns at the heads of the principal streets. One member of the strike committee urged angrily that the workers take advantage of their numbers to overpower the police and turn the machine guns around. To Muste's relief, the other committee members pointed out that the guns had been *meant* to provoke the strikers into violence that would discredit their movement. "They can't weave wool with machine guns," observed one of the calmer rebels.

The decision of the strike committee—none of whose members had heard of Gandhi—was announced to a hall filled with workers. Many of those in the audience, including women, had been clubbed. Many were worrying about their children for whom they couldn't afford to buy shoes. A split on the issue of nonviolence could have destroyed the strike. Muste told the crowd that any violence by the workers would be self-defeating.

"What we must do," the young minister said, "is smile as we pass the machine guns and the police." He spoke grimly and added, looking hard into the hall, "I trust that those of you who are spies for the employers will dutifully report that this is going to be our policy." The crowd laughed, and there was no further danger of disunity. "That incident," Muste said many years later, "and several others in which I've since been involved have made me certain that Americans are just as capable of understanding and applying nonviolent resistance as Indians."

In Lawrence, nonviolent resistance was made more difficult because of the confusions caused within the ranks of the strikers by labor spies. Muste, for example, discovered that the committee member who had suggested shooting down the police was in the employ of the millowners. Later, the financial secretary of the strike committee turned out to be a hireling of a detective agency working for the employers. He was about to leave Lawrence with the relief money at a time when strikers' morale was again sinking. The financial secretary felt impelled, however, to tell Muste and the other ministers from the Comradeship what he was going to do. "I'm finally convinced," he said when they met at a private rendezvous at the edge of town, "that you guys are on the level. When you first came to Lawrence, I figured you must be secret agents of somebody in the ownership setup. Otherwise what would three preachers be doing all mixed up in a strike?"

The spy also told Muste that the local powers planned to indict the preacher for murder. Several weeks before, a man had been killed at a strikers' relief station as the result of a private feud, but the authorities intended to claim that the murder had been caused by strike agitation and that, accordingly, the leading outside agitator was responsible for the death. Muste claims he was not surprised that the undercover agent had risked his own security to warn him of the plot. "After all, the ability of human beings in one capacity to perform acts they would abhor in another, to show understanding and mercy in one situation while performing horrible atrocities in another is seen frequently. An example is the behavior of sensible people, including Christians and other believers, in time of war."

Two years later, when Muste had become General Secretary of the Amalgamated Textile Workers of America, the same free-lance espionage agent applied for a job as a spy against the employers. Muste declined to discuss the matter with him.

The plan to charge Muste with murder never materialized, but it did begin to appear as if the Lawrence strike would fail. Funds were low, and the police were terrorizing more and more of the strike leaders. Muste escaped one beating because he was out of the city on a night when detectives burst into his hotel room. The millowners meanwhile were tempting their errant employees by offering an increase in piece rates in return for the cut in the work week from fifty-four to forty-eight hours—with a further provision that no shop grievance committee would be recognized. The strike had lasted fifteen weeks, and the strike committee decided it would be unfair to ask the workers to endure more. They expected that the majority of the strikers would accept the companies' offer.

Several weeks before the strike neared collapse, Muste had gone to a New York convention of textile workers from Lawrence, New York, Paterson, Passaic, and a couple of other mill towns. The delegates had set up the Amalgamated Textile Workers of America, and Muste, because of his reputation as leader of the Lawrence strike, was appointed secretary. He returned to Lawrence, and was soon convinced that he had lost that particular battle. One afternoon, Muste mournfully left for the railroad station on the way back to New York. He felt he had to prepare the other locals of the new union for the shock of the Lawrence defeat. Muste was intercepted by an emissary from the head of the American Woolen Company Mills asking for a meeting.

When Muste and the millowner met in the yard of the owner's home, the latter began railing at Muste as "the outside agitator who has brought all this needless trouble and suffering to Lawrence."

Muste, weary, asked: "Is this what you brought me here for?"

"No. How can we settle this damn strike?"

As Muste later discovered, the millowners were beginning to get orders again, and decided it was to their economic advantage to yield. Apparently their undercover information service had not told them the workers were themselves about to surrender. Muste informed the strike committee that the owners were willing to meet their terms which included a 12-percent increase in hour and piece rates and recognition of shop grievance committees in all departments. The next night, Muste remembers, "There was a great outdoor mass meeting. The strikers as a body formally ratified the settlement and authorized those who were needed to put the machinery back in operation after a sixteen weeks' layoff to return to work the next morning. They sang:

'Arise, ye prisoners of starvation . . .
We have been nought; we shall be all.'

"And that was that."

Muste was now a full-time labor leader. Because of his work in the Lawrence strike, he had asked to be released from his agreement with the Quakers in Providence. In 1960, on his seventy-fifth birthday, the Providence Monthly Meeting of Friends recalled that occasion in a letter to Muste. "We have been thinking about thee," a member wrote, "with much affection as we read through the early minutes of our Meeting." The present clerk of the Providence Monthly Meeting added: "Only a few of the present members remember thy services to our Meeting at a time when thee needed us and we needed thee. At that time thee had made a courageous and difficult decision—to devote thy life to the cause of peace—and thee has never turned back."

"A. J. Muste," the minutes of September 28, 1918, read, "asks to be released to be of service to textile workers in Lawrence. He expresses his appreciation to Providence Monthly Meeting, his embarrassment at not fulfilling his agreement, but feels led to this service among the textile workers. The Meeting felt he should be released and expressed regret at his going and appreciation for his service."

"That Lawrence strike," observes Roger Baldwin, who for many years was head of the American Civil Liberties Union, "was especially significant because it was one of the first examples of collective, pacifist pro-labor activity led by ministers." In his book, *American Protestantism and Social Issues: 1919-1939* (University of North Carolina Press), Dr. Robert Moats Miller notes: "The gaunt, raw-boned, 'Fool-for-Christ' Muste . . . won for the workers and thus began an association with labor unparalleled by that of any other cleric."

6

BROOKWOOD
LABOR
COLLEGE

*"Make Up Your Mind and Act, While
Action Will Have Some Meaning."*

THE Amalgamated Textile Workers of America was
assisted by Sidney Hillman's Amalgamated Clothing
Workers of America, a militant industrial union. Muste,
in fact, set up headquarters at the ACWA's national office in New York, but technically his union was not
affiliated with Hillman's because the latter did not want
to jeopardize his own organization until the textile
workers had proved themselves. For over two years,
Muste was a vigorous organizer. "I do not recall," he
says, "a week when there was not a strike on somewhere
in our union, which before long embraced locals as far
west as Chicago and in neighboring towns in southern
Wisconsin. There was no strike without labor spies; no
strike in which we did not encounter arbitrary, and
usually violent, conduct on the part of the police; no
strike, hardly even a union meeting in those days, where
raids by Attorney General Palmer's men were not carried out or at least threatened."

Muste became expert at dealing with the labor spies.

56

"They'd always be there heckling and trying to start arguments at a strike meeting or at a picket line." Invariably, Muste warned leading members of the strike committees to look out for the spies and to avoid violent retaliation and its resultant uproar. "I told them to play it cool, so to speak," he has explained. "And when I was at a meeting, I'd tell the hecklers right out, 'You people are evidently spies sent here by the company, but we will not be diverted. You may stay if you like, however.' " Muste chuckles, "A couple of times they actually got up and walked out."

Muste was occasionally jailed. There were other problems, as at a Passaic, New Jersey, meeting during which Norman Thomas, speaking of the civil liberties due strikers, began reading the Declaration of Independence. The police turned out the lights. "This consigning of the Declaration of Independence to outer darkness," Thomas' voice came from the platform, "is exactly what is happening in Passaic."

For all his persistent work, Muste did not have much success with the Amalgamated Textile Workers of America. There was a depression; and in fact nine months after the Lawrence strike had been won, the mills there closed down because they had no orders. It was during this discouraging period that Muste's was one of the American unions invited to send delegates or at least official observers to Moscow for a proposed Red International of Labor Unions. Muste declined. "Since we had not been able to build a viable organization at home, why pretend we had any title to a role in building any kind of world organization? Maneuvering with what amounted to paper organizations (a practice to which Communists have regrettably been addicted) always reminds me of the fact that one of the very first unions in British labor history, a union with only a handful of members even there, was known as the Grand National Consolidated Union of Great Britain, Ireland, and the World."

Muste's pragmatism has always been characteristic of his work during all his various ideological turns. In August, 1960, for example, Muste helped arrange a conference in France of theologians, including several from Eastern Europe. The meeting, the third of these "Puidoux Conferences" in recent years, was held to explore ways in which the churches of both power blocs could help prevent war. "A.J.," observed a London curate in attendance, "constantly kept the young theoreticians from letting go of reality."

In the summer of 1921, Muste, thirty-six, realistically resigned as General Secretary of the Amalgamated Textile Workers of America. His new post was Educational Director of Brookwood Labor College in Katonah, forty-one miles north of New York. Several of the more militant labor leaders had concluded that a full-scale school for potential union leaders had become essential. A sizable percentage of the young strike leaders had been forced to stop their education after the eighth grade, were recent immigrants, or the children of recent immigrants, and needed to learn more about the theory and practice of labor militancy. Brookwood Labor College was to provide its students with the broad historical background of the labor movement as well as specific tools, such as instruction in keeping minutes, writing resolutions, organizing strikes, setting up relief organizations, and other techniques in the economic power struggle.

The Brookwood grounds had previously been used for two years as a progressive Christian Socialist school for children directed by William and Helen Fincke. The Finckes were pacifists and members of the Fellowship of Reconciliation. When they decided their property would be more useful to the general welfare as a labor school for adults, they initiated a conference of union leaders and educators that resulted in the founding of Brookwood Labor College.

From the school's start, the hierarchy of the American Federation of Labor was suspicious of Brookwood, because many of the faculty were not only oriented toward Socialism in various forms but also advocated a broad industrial workers' movement in contrast to the AFL's narrower concern with craft unions.

Brookwood, the first resident school for workers in the country, was independent of AFL politics although it received support from several unions affiliated with the AFL. These unions provided promising workers with scholarships to the school in the hope that their members would return better equipped to work in the labor movement. The initial class of nineteen assembled in October, 1921. At first, full-time students enrolled for a two-year course in the social sciences, and others came for summer institutes. After three years, the regular course was reduced to one year, although a student could return after spending an interval at home in active union work.

Cara Cook, a teacher at Brookwood in later years, wrote an unpublished history of the school in which she quotes a charter member of the faculty as saying that "everyone who came here the first year, even as visitors, was pressed into service. Before he had his first meal, he was expected to cut up enough wood for the fires." The instructor of social problems peeled potatoes, and students scrubbed floors between reading assignments. Faculty and student body also took care of the school livestock, and worked in the fields. Gradually, the faculty did less extracurricular work, but the students continued to be expected to help with the chores. Since several were professional carpenters, painters, and plumbers, the school was able to economize on running expenses through the presence of so handy a student body. The average age of the students during Muste's twelve years as director was twenty-one to thirty although there were often several who were older.

At its height, Brookwood was supported by thirteen national and international unions. There were also grants from the American Fund for Public Service, established by Charles Garland who had inherited a million dollars from his father, a broker, in 1919, and had at first refused the inheritance. Garland believed property to be a social product that should be used for the benefit of society. He was not, however, an advocate of social change by force and declared himself a non-resistant. "I have faith in the law of love. A man's giving up should be purely voluntary." Garland was finally persuaded to accept the inheritance and give it up voluntarily by establishing a fund. During its existence (1921-41), the fund was administered by a board of liberals with widely divergent views. In the twenties, grants were made to the labor and radical press, for strike relief and protection of minorities, and for research studies in these and other fields. A major beneficiary of the fund's concern with labor education was Brookwood.

Throughout his term at the school, Muste himself raised several hundred thousand dollars. He has always been a prodigious fund raiser. Starting in Boston during the First World War, Muste came to know several relatively wealthy pacifists who would contribute to causes he recommended. His list of potential donors has grown through the years, and he is still usually able to produce enough money whenever one of his various projects is in crisis. An associate explains Muste's technique: "He approaches rich people on the basis that they have something which they're privileged to share with the movement, and he is going to provide them with just that privilege."

Muste is persistent. He may write to the same source again and again. Occasionally, however, he is sent an unsolicited check and told to use the money where he thinks it can be most effective. "I started out," Muste has said concerning his prowess as a fund raiser, "with a great aversion to asking for money, and I still feel diffident about it. I sometimes thought people would give me money if only because they would sympathize with my embarrassment. Through the years, however, I came to know several people who had confidence in my integrity and believed that a cause for which I appealed would be what it appeared to be." Muste's record of success is comforting to his associates. An editor of *Liberation,* the monthly journal to which Muste has devoted considerable energy in recent years, is not dismayed at the fact that the publication, now in its fourth year, is often in financial difficulty. "As long as A.J. is around," he observes, "there'll always be a *Liberation.*"

As fund raiser, coordinator and teacher, Muste thrived at Brookwood. After the first year, the student body generally numbered around forty each term. "They all worked so hard," says Helen Norton Starr, who was a faculty member. "The beauty of teaching there was that everybody had such a strong desire to learn. And there were no grades, no report cards. It was an ideal situation for a teacher. When I was the librarian, for example, I actually had to chase the students out of the library at closing time."

The backgrounds of the students were quite diversified. There were miners from Ohio, Illinois, Pennsylvania, and West Virginia, as well as garment workers and representatives of the building trades and the railroads. "They ranged culturally," Muste recalls, "from devout church members from isolated and backward villages to extremely sophisticated people who read Marx and the Russian novelists, attended Provincetown Playhouse in New York and saw the O'Neill plays before they came to Broadway, saved pennies to get standing-room admission to the Metropolitan Opera House, and went to avant-garde dances in Greenwich Village on weekends."

One young Pennsylvania miner, a Catholic, was shocked by Muste's course in the history of civilization. "If what I'm being told here is the truth," he told Muste after class one afternoon, "everything I have believed is a lie." "I told him," says Muste, "not to take anything on anybody's mere say-so, to keep on thinking for himself. We, on our part, did not want to tell him, or anybody else what to think. I also suggested that he write his priest or talk to him when he went home for the holidays. Later, he did talk with the priest, and what the priest told him must have reassured him, for he developed into a self-assured, highly intelligent student."

In addition to history of civilization, Muste taught courses in social problems, modern social history, labor problems, American history, and the history of American and foreign labor movements. Several Brookwood alumni recall a recurring Muste credo: "What matters most is the *direction* in which you are now. You may be approaching a position for a long time. When you take it, it may seem sudden, but it isn't really."

Cara Cook emphasizes that "A.J. was always an actionist. He'd listen patiently to the students discussing a problem for hours, but when he thought they had become paralyzed in talk, he'd interrupt and say firmly, 'Make up your mind and act, while action will have some meaning.' "

Three decades later, in 1958, four members of the Committee for Nonviolent Action were in Honolulu preparing a journey of protest on the ketch, *Golden Rule,* into the nuclear testing area around the Marshall Islands. They delayed sailing while arguing whether to wait for the result of a Federal Court action in which their plans had involved them. Muste, who had been involved in the preparations for the voyage and had volunteered to be one of the crewmen, finally told the demonstrators, "Sail or go to jail. But do *something!*"

"As always in his life," Helen Norton Starr says, "A.J. had a remarkably equable temperament during his years at Brookwood, but inaction could turn on the neon lights in him. He once strode out of a student meeting that had been deadlocked for hours. He was in such an obvious state of irritation that he left the students gasping. They had become so accustomed to being able to argue with poppa forever."

Most of the time, however, Muste was a benevolent center of authority. He often read aloud, usually during the Friday night social programs. Shakespeare was a frequent choice, and another favorite was Stephen Vincent Benét's *John Brown's Body.* Muste also enjoyed acting out the parts in Milt Gross's "Nize Baby" and was adept at other varieties of humorous monologues. Former students remember a parody of "To Be or Not to Be" that Muste has since performed at parties, meetings of the War Resisters League, and in other widely divergent contexts.

Muste's sense of the absurd has remained with him through all his roles in and out of the church. James Bristol of the American Friends Service Committee observes, "I have seen A.J. laugh so hard, on a platform as well as in private conversation, that he couldn't complete what he was trying to say." Muste can also be drily effective in speeding up meetings. During an enervating wrangle about parliamentary procedure one late night in early 1963, Muste finally observed, "The chair does not understand all this byplay." He paused. "Nor does the chair care." The argument was at an end.

At Brookwood, Muste did much to relieve the inevitable tensions that resulted from an unusually volatile group of students and teachers working very closely together in a small area for months at a time. He was both the head of the court of appeals at Brookwood and a fantasy father for several students and faculty members. "When he went away for days or weeks of lectures or labor organizing," a former student says, "we'd look forward so much to his return, partly because he told such vivid stories about his travels and partly because it was just reassuring to have him back." Cara Cook adds that "A.J. was continually calling in students and staff members and listening for hours and hours to their personal problems. He furthered a number of romances at Brookwood, and saw that they were corrected or consummated. He was so understanding and yet objective that he could make most of us open up."

"The best way I can describe his effect," Helen Norton Starr says, "is that he had charismatic qualities. He was an incisive intellectual with a remarkable ability to analyze a complex situation, but he was also a warm, witty man of great personal charm."

The surrounding Katonah community, part of wealthy, conservative Westchester County, continually speculated about this unprecedented school on the steep hill outside of town. Its director, a minister who didn't hold services, at least had children. At first there were the two Muste girls, Nancy and Connie. When the school opened, Nancy was six and Connie was two. Muste believes that Nancy particularly helped relieve at least some of the villagers' fears concerning the character of the school. "We sent her to public school in the village. Most mornings, she rode down there in the sidecar of an instructor's motorcycle. Since we had the reputation, as did the school which had preceded the labor colony, of being 'red,' there were suspicions that we must be a 'free-love colony.' One look at Nancy was enough to dispel any such notions and to convince all who were not dead set against being convinced that there must be some nice people up there on the hill."

Later, a third child, John, was born. "A.J. came striding into a student meeting soon after his son was born," Cara Cook remembers, "with a huge smile. The students gave him a big hand." Like his sisters, John was a lively, cheerful child. One faculty member recalls a rhetorical question-game John used to play with whomever he met on the campus.

"Which party are *you* for?" the child would ask. "The Socialist Party or the Lovestonite Party?" Without waiting for an answer, the boy would giggle, *"I'm* for a *birthday* party."

In time the villagers came to know people from the school, and became somewhat reassured that the radicals on the hill were normal in deportment, if not in their ideas. "I talked to a woman's group once," says Helen Norton Starr, "and told them I supposed there was talk that Brookwood was a center of free love. Actually, I assured them, we were drearily respectable. All the faculty members lived with their own wives. There was tittering in the audience. I found out later that there had indeed been a 'free love' scandal in the town—in the local high school."

By 1928, young Brookwood staff members were successfully collecting clothing from the townspeople for
the relief of striking miners in West Virginia. "I even,"
says one, "tackled the notoriously tough Westchester
County Building Trades Council, and collected a heap-
ing truckload of clothing as well as a promise to send
money."

"Essentially, however," notes Cara Cook, "we remained queer from the point of view of the local citi-
zenry, although a few liberal old ladies did help arrange
meetings between us and the villagers in the local
church. A.J. himself did become respected in the coun-
tryside; but, since the school was set apart from everything else, I wasn't surprised that as soon as Brookwood
finally closed down, a rezoning law was passed which
made it impossible for there ever again to be a school
in that section of Katonah."

Until 1928, Brookwood continued to grow in importance. Under Muste's direction, it was concerned with
what he termed a "factual" approach to labor problems.
In 1923, he had declared: "We would have the organized workers confront every situation not with preju-
dices, superstitions, mere notions or feelings, personal
animus, but with the willingness to seek out the facts
and to base judgment and action on the facts. If we
negotiate with employers, let us not go with opinions or
'hot air,' but armed with facts. When a town is to be
organized, let us proceed not by guesswork, but with
careful knowledge about the place, its workers, their
conditions." Similarly, although Muste did not in the
least intend Brookwood to be aloof from internal union
disagreements, he wanted his students to know the
"facts, economic, social, psychological" underlying the
warring views. "The man with 'right' tendencies who

goes out of Brookwood thinking that every 'left' is necessarily a destructive fool, or the man with 'left' tendencies who goes out thinking a 'right' is merely a yellow coward, has utterly failed to get the Brookwood point of view."

As the school developed, however, the "facts" increasingly led Muste and his supporters among the faculty to the conviction that the American Federation of Labor was moving too slowly and was overly "right." Moreover, Muste believed that the school's fact-finding function did not exclude Brookwood from taking an active part in the labor movement. "Geographically, we were off in a somewhat idyllic country setting, and the students were away from their jobs and day-to-day union activities. But psychologically, we were participants in the economic and political movements of that time. Students continued to attend local union meetings if their homes were near enough. Others might travel farther if there was a crucial policy decision to be made in their unions, or a strike in progress."

Muste himself was elected a Vice-President of the American Federation of Teachers in 1923, and became a member of the executive committee of the Workers Education Bureau, the official educational wing of the AFL. (Brookwood, however, remained independent of the bureau's direction.) He wrote regularly for labor publications, and contributed leading articles to *Labor Age,* the monthly organ of the Labor Publication Society, which eventually became a center of opposition to the AFL leaders. Muste was a member of the Board of Directors of that society. After 1926, *Labor Age* pressed for organization of the mass-production industries. A leader in this campaign for industrial unionism which led to the formation of the Congress of Industrial

Organizations in the 1930's, Muste had been complaining throughout the preceding decade that the AFL was "wedded to an arbitrary idea of craft unionism."

Though increasingly convinced that Marxism was an exceptionally useful analytic method, Muste mistrusted the Communist Party. There were some Communists at Brookwood, and others came to speak. Muste recalls a visit by William Z. Foster, who had recently returned from his first trip to Moscow: "One of the questions in the minds of all labor activists at that time was whether Bill had joined the Communist Party. He sought to create the impression that he had not. I have carried with me all through the years a vivid recollection of that day nearly forty years ago. I have lived it over again at fairly frequent intervals since. It was a feeling of uneasiness, certainly not of hostility in the personal sense. I felt there was a human being inside him, but that it was under restraint, hidden somewhere. The element of straightforwardness was now lacking. There he was, over there, and here was I. It would remain so."

In 1924, Muste worked hard for the presidential campaign of Robert M. La Follette, Sr., of Wisconsin. Running on the third-party ticket of the newly formed Progressive Party, La Follette was strongly pro-labor. He particularly appealed to Muste because he had voted against America's entry into the war. Muste made several speeches for La Follette in the Midwest, including one at Holland, Michigan.

Muste hadn't been back to Holland since his graduation from Hope College in 1905. "Since then I had committed a whole series of crimes, such as getting fired from a church for my pacifism, getting arrested on the picket line in a strike, and haranguing strike meetings in a plain shirt and without a tie. There was a good turnout at the meeting and a friendly reception. The head of the English department, who had once regarded me as his star protégé, refused to attend. The next day he did make a concession, as I was later informed, saying that he was pleased to learn that I had not 'ranted, but talked common sense—more or less.' "

A nephew of Muste, Arthur C. Johnson, now a minister in the Midwest, admits that disappointment in Muste's own family and among Dutch Reformed elders with Muste's post-Michigan career continued into the next decade. "When I was about twelve I was told that he had a brilliant mind (a 'deep' mind our Dutch people in the Midwest termed it) and that at a young age he had already commanded large churches and good pulpits. Yet he had left the 'church of his fathers.' Even when I was older and entered Hope College, whenever my relationship to A.J. was mentioned to former mentors of his, I sensed a feeling of tragedy that he had left the church. The consensus was that he could have had a brilliant career as a professor at a college or a seminary. As I got to know A.J. in my more mature years, however, I have come to see him in a different light. His very brilliance caused him to see that truth is something to be done, not just something to believe."

In that 1924 election, La Follette came in third, polling 17 percent of the vote. Muste was encouraged, but the American Federation of Labor, which had abandoned its usual nonpartisanship to endorse La Follette, was distinctly discouraged, and refused to support any further plans for a labor party.

Muste was, in any case, less and less impressed by the AFL leadership. In 1924, William Green succeeded Samuel Gompers as President of the Federation. To Muste, "Green was to the labor movement what Calvin Coolidge was to the American political scene—an incarnation of perfect mediocrity." The AFL became even more cautious under Green, and according to Muste, "entered upon a period of stodgy class-collaboration." Green and his colleagues in turn regarded Muste and the Brookwood Labor College with gathering distrust.

On August 7, 1928, the executive council of the American Federation of Labor, basing its decision on an unpublished report by Vice-President Matthew Woll, advised all its affiliates to withdraw support from Brookwood. Woll had reportedly become convinced that the school was encouraging anti-AFL and antireligious attitudes, and had also been the scene of pro-Soviet demonstrations. At the 1928 AFL convention, Muste was denied the floor to appeal the Woll report, which had still not been released, and the convention approved the decision of the executive council. On January 18, 1929, Muste was removed from the executive council of the Workers Educational Bureau.

Reviewing the AFL's condemnation of Brookwood, Muste recalls wryly that "one specific allegation was that at a May Day observance at the school the picture of Samuel Gompers had been displayed along with those of Eugene V. Debs, Marx, and Lenin. This was true. The composition of the student body being what it was, some of them were as irked by having Gompers' picture on the wall as others were by Lenin's, but it was in accord with the catholicity we observed in these matters that both were there and that the whole student body took part in the meeting. We were given to understand that in the eyes of the AFL magnates the fact that Gompers' picture, like the others, had a border of red ribbon around it constituted an additional affront."

The Young Workers League (a Communist group) meanwhile warned *its* members to stay away from Brookwood: "Brookwood is no more Communist in spirit than the Executive Board of the A.F.L. itself. We have always found that this institution has consistently functioned as a cloak for . . . the reactionary labor fakers . . . the Y.W.L. will continue its struggle against Brookwood and its ideology and will make every effort to destroy whatever influence it may have among the working youth."

The *Daily Worker* added righteously that Brookwood's "teachings are known to be those primarily of class collaboration," and "its fate at the hands of the executive council is one more demonstration that those who stand neither with the right nor with the left get the bricks from both extremes." Around this time, a young lady Communist from Chicago, who was attending Brookwood, took the curtains from her room back home with her. Brookwood, after all, was a capitalist institution, and the curtains belonged to the workers.

As for the AFL's charges that Brookwood nurtured antireligious doctrines, labor historian James O. Morris, in a carefully detailed study of Brookwood in his book, *Conflict Within the AFL* (Cornell University Press), concludes that although evolution was taught in the school, "the college did not directly attack religion. . . . On the contrary, persons of all faiths were accepted as students and transportation was furnished to those who wished to attend the church at Katonah."

Muste himself had "put his religion in his pocket," in a faculty member's phrase, "out of deference to the nonreligious people at Brookwood. There was no preaching and no saying of grace, but there was certainly no attacking by him of religion. I would say, however, that by that time the labor movement itself had become a religion to A.J."

Several unions and educators continued to support Brookwood despite the AFL's excommunication order.

Student enrollment did not decline markedly until 1932, when the Depression made it impossible for many unions to keep up their worker scholarships. Muste's own departure in 1933 was caused less by external pressures than by a serious split which had developed within the faculty itself concerning his labor and political activities outside the school and his conception of Brookwood's role in the labor movement.

7

THE
DETOUR
TO THE LEFT

*"I Chose Revolution, Recognizing That It
Might Involve Violence."*

DURING the years at Brookwood, Muste had become
more and more of a revolutionary. "In 1928," he recalls,
"I still thought of myself as a Christian, though I was
not particularly active in any church or even in the
Quaker Meeting to which I belonged, or as a pacifist.
In politics, I voted for the Socialist Party candidates
without being a party member, largely because I could
never get up much enthusiasm for electoral activity, as
against education on the one hand and direct labor
struggles in the economic field on the other. I had begun
a running battle with the Communist Party, which was
to last for years, chiefly because I felt that the party's
policies in the trade-union field were usually inept, con-
trived and disruptive. A few years later, I had become
a Trotskyist Marxist-Leninist and had accordingly
ceased to think of myself as a Christian and a pacifist."

In the late 1920's, Muste began for the first time to investigate extensively the works of Marx, Trotsky, and
Lenin. Earlier in the decade, his reading had been

mainly of historians such as Beard and Spengler, Socialists such as G. D. H. Cole, and the initial sociologists and social psychologists. Muste eventually turned to the revolutionaries, as he had in 1915 to the writings of the mystics, "not out of academic interest, but because I faced conditions and problems about which I felt I had to make a decision. The result of the reading was in each case *acted out* rather than written about."

Even though many Protestant preachers and their congregations had by 1928 become sympathetic to pacifism as part of their revulsion against the First World War, Muste's faith in the church as an agent of social change was slim. His confidence in the church had been severely shaken by the nearly unanimous support it had given to the war and to the persecution of the few pacifist preachers in the war years. He also felt, as he wrote in his autobiographical notes for *Liberation,* that "the churches were identified with the *status quo.* They were middle class in composition and coloration. With rare exceptions, they seemed irrelevant. Furthermore, when you looked out on the scene of misery and desperation during the Depression, you saw that it was the radicals, the Left-wingers, the people who had adopted some form of Marxian philosophy, who were *doing something* about the situation, who were banding people together for action, who were putting up a fight. Unless you were indifferent or despairing, you lined up with them. It must also be said that in many cases these doers and fighters were Communists or those set in motion by them. So far as my experience goes, in any specific situation where there was a militant non-Communist Left, it could stand up to them, in spite of the often vicious tactics used by the Communist Party. But if there was a vacuum, the Communist filled it. Without them the unions in the mass-production industries would not have been built.

"It was also on the Left—and here again the Communists cannot be excluded—that one found people who were truly 'religious' in the sense that they were virtually completely committed. They were betting their lives on the cause they embraced. Often they gave up ordinary comforts, security, life itself, with a burning devotion which few Christians display toward the Christ whom they profess as Lord and incarnation of God. Later I was to mourn the wastage of so much youthful devotion, and its corruption among Communists and others, which I had witnessed from the inside."

Muste's pacifism also appeared irrelevant to him in those years. "I came to embrace the view that only revolutionary action by the working class and other elements under the leadership of a vanguard party could bring in a new social order, and that revolutionary action did not in principle exclude violence. Violence in taking over power would almost certainly be necessary and hence justified. Also, the effort to apply Gandhian methods to American conditions had scarcely begun at that time. Pacifism was mostly a middle-class and an individualistic phenomenon. The churches certainly were not giving illustrations of spiritual force, of true community, which might have had a nonviolent but transforming influence. For a time, I tried to reconcile my Christian pacifism with involvement in the struggle as it was then taking place. Gradually, as I said to someone in that period, I came to feel that I was more and more a caricature of a Christian pacifist and only a half-baked revolutionary, and that I had to choose. I chose revolution, recognizing that it might involve violence. I did not, having given up my pacifism, think that I could remain a Christian."

As usual, having gradually reached a new position, Muste was self-impelled to *"experience* ideas, rather than just think them." His move toward becoming a revolutionary was accelerated by his major role in founding the Conference for Progressive Labor Action at a convention in the Presbyterian Labor Temple in New York on May 25-26, 1929. Ten years later, after one more radical change in his beliefs, Muste was to become director of that Temple.

The C.P.L.A. called for industrial unions; the end of all forms of discrimination within unions; the establishment of unemployed benefits and other forms of social insurance; and a five-day week. The "Musteites," as C.P.L.A. members soon were called, also urged the formation of a Labor Party, recognition of the Soviet Union, and a "definitely anti-imperialist, anti-militarist and internationalist labor movement."

The conference was attended by 151 delegates from 31 cities in 18 states. They were organizing, labor historian James Morris has pointed out, "the first body whose basic and avowed purpose was to reform the American Federation of Labor from within. About two-thirds of those present were reported to be active trade unionists, the others were representatives of the Socialist party and 'friends' of organized labor." Norman Thomas, for example, was on the executive board. *Labor Age* became the movement's official journal, and A. J. Muste became chairman of C.P.L.A.

The American Federation of Labor did not feel it required reforming, especially from within. The C.P.L.A. was charged with the most noxious of all labor sins, fostering "dual unionism." The AFL's *Weekly News Service* observed sardonically that C.P.L.A. was "blessed by those who believe they have a divine commission to lead the workers." Leading the C.P.L.A., moreover, was a "group of professional tingling souls who dream of a Labor Party." The Communists jeered with equal fervor. William Z. Foster termed the Musteites "little brothers of the big labor fakirs." More to the point, Foster realized that he was being threatened by " 'left' Social-Democrats" who intended to form a party to rival his own. Within the C.P.L.A. itself, there was further tension between the Musteites and representatives of the Socialist Party; and in 1932, the Muste forces, who believed violence might be necessary to overthrow capitalism, forced the Socialist members out of the Conference.

Increasingly, several Brookwood faculty members and students became convinced that Muste was using the school as an arm of the C.P.L.A. and was devoting too much of his time to C.P.L.A. activities. Helen Norton Starr, who was to become part of the opposition to Muste at Brookwood, recognized that "temperamentally, he had reached the stage at which he *had* to get into the middle of labor action. He had to go out and rattle the can. His interests clearly were shifting away from Brookwood, and he spent more and more time lecturing outside the school and helping unions in the East and the South in organization and strike work."

National headquarters for the C.P.L.A. were opened in New York on June 10, 1929. In the next three years, there were at least seventeen branches in key industrial centers such as Detroit, Chicago, Cleveland, Pittsburgh, Youngstown, and Philadelphia. Among the strikes the C.P.L.A. joined were the brutal labor wars in the textile mills of Marion, North Carolina, in July, 1929. Working and living conditions for the workers there were primitive. In July, 650 employees of the Baldwin mills in Marion left work. Officials of their union, the United Textile Workers, did not want a strike because there were no funds for relief. Also in town advising the workers was Alfred Hoffman, a Hosiery Workers representative and Brookwood graduate, who also worried about the lack of funds and tried to dissuade 1,500 workers from the Clinchfield mills from joining the others. Further complicating the Marion situation was the presence of a militant strategist from C.P.L.A.

The Clinchfield management precipitated a strike at its plant by firing a hundred union members and locking out the rest early in August. When the plant was reopened, mass picketing began, and by early September, state troops had taken over the town and smashed the strike. The troops were withdrawn after a labor-management conference reached an oral agreement under which the work week was cut to fifty-five hours with a proportionate decrease in pay. Management agreed to rehire the strikers, except for twelve at the Baldwin mill. The employers reneged on the antidiscrimination clause of the agreement, however, and blacklisted a hundred strikers. The night shift at Baldwin walked out on October 2. In a melee on the road before the front gate of the plant, the strikers tried to persuade the day shift to go home. Police threw tear gas. A 65-year-old striker, a cripple, blinded and panicked by the gas, grappled with the sheriff, was beaten to the ground, and while on his hands and knees, was shot. The police opened fire on the rest. At least four died, all shot in the back. No deputies or mill officials were injured.

A funeral service was held on the morning of October 4. No local minister would officiate. All were afraid of the millowners. Reverend James Myers, Secretary of the Federal Council of Churches, and Reverend A. J. Muste conducted the services. A few local strike leaders and an official of the United Textile Workers also spoke. In the middle of the service, an old, bearded mountain preacher, Cicero Queens, suddenly came out of the crowd and jumped onto the platform where the bodies of the dead lay. He fell on his knees, raised his arms straight into the air, and prayed:

> O Lord Jesus Christ, here are men in their coffins, blood of my blood, bone of my bone. I trust, O God, that these friends will go to a place better than this mill village or any other place in Carolina. O God, we know we are not in high society, but we know Jesus Christ loves us. The poor people have their rights too. For the work we do in this world, is that what we get if we demand our rights? Jesus Christ, your son, O God, was a working man. If He were to pass under these trees today, He would see these cold bodies lying here before us. O God, mend the broken hearts of these loved ones left behind. Dear God, do feed their children. Drive selfishness and cruelty out of your world. Dear God—what would Jesus do if he were to come to Carolina?

Cicero Queens walked away. One millowner, L. L. Jenkins, was also present, and said, "What I am today and all that I have I owe to people like you, to the men and women who for forty years have stood faithfully by the spindle and loom. . . . You are my people. I love you." The workers were not demonstrably moved.

All but one of the bodies were taken away for burial elsewhere. The last of the dead was to be interred in a run-down cemetery next to the Baldwin mill. Muste and several others followed the coffin. As it was being lowered, the undertaker asked if a minister were present. There was silence. Muste took off his hat, stepped up to the open grave, and said: "We consecrate this worker's body and give it back to the earth from which it came. He has fought a good fight in a noble cause. He will rest in peace."

Also representative of the kind of activity that was taking Muste away from his Brookwood classes was an expedition to Washington a couple of years later under the auspices of the People's Lobby of which John Dewey had become president. The Lobby was petitioning President Hoover to devise means of dealing with the deepening Depression. A number of labor leaders, educators, and Socialists composed the delegation which was to present a petition to Hoover.

Edmund Wilson, who was there, described the "lean Netherlander who resembles a country schoolmaster and stands in the posture of a preacher, his hands clasped in front of him and his head tilted back, looking down his long nose through his spectacles with an expression at once dreamy and shrewd . . . A. J. Muste has taken more responsibility than most of the persons present; he has followed with close attention the reading of the drafted memorial, and brought to bear on it a lucid intelligence, with a tincture of ironic humor, rather European than American. He withdraws with someone else to condense it and make the language more accurate."

The best the committee could do that day was to leave the petition with Hoover's secretary. It was one of many times before and since that Muste has been involved in drawing up, editing, and rewriting statements and resolutions. Although his own writing style is often diffuse, he has a quick eye for prolixity in others.

Mark Starr, who at the time was on the Brookwood faculty and later became educational director of the International Ladies Garment Workers Union, recalls Muste returning from such forays as the trip to Washington and describing his defeats "almost with a certain glee, a glee that came from his unabated enjoyment in the actual participation, in *doing* something. The man has always thrived on opposition, and enjoys the very techniques and processes of tactical and ideological battles. At Brookwood, he would have felt terribly constricted if he had had to remain solely in the classroom."

Robert Moats Miller, in chronicling the events of the period in *American Protestantism and Social Issues, 1919-1939,* writes of another textile strike, a 1931 struggle in Paterson. New Jersey. "A. J. Muste, as usual, was on hand, a battle-scarred veteran of a hundred strikes." Muste and a few other clergymen, Miller continued, "were marching around the mill with the pickets like Israel about Jericho when they were arrested and politely escorted into patrol wagons."

Muste was beginning to show the strain of trying to combine the careers of educator and labor agitator. Brookwood meanwhile was losing enrollment because of the Depression; decisions had to be made about which faculty members would be dropped; and resentment concerning Muste's outside activities was mounting. There was the additional feeling that Muste, had he concentrated on Brookwood, could have raised more money to make up the growing deficit. "A. J. became even thinner than usual," Mark Starr remembers, "and he was constantly drawn tight—like a wire about to snap."

Starr had become one of Muste's opponents in the faculty split. "A.J. and those who supported him," Starr summarizes, "wanted Brookwood as a whole to be more actively involved in union work. Their faction proposed increasing the number of extension courses and even selling the Brookwood property with the intent of settling the school in a less expensive location in an industrial center. We, however, believed that Brookwood's major contribution was as an educational force. We didn't want the school to lose its unique character by becoming too closely identified with any one group in labor, such as the C.P.L.A. We also did not believe, as A.J. did, that the labor movement needed another party. A.J. was convinced that the Communist Party had failed and that a new center for the progressive left to come was needed. Accordingly, he was working hard to build the C.P.L.A. as a nucleus for that party; but in the process, Brookwood was losing opportunities to get labor support from other sources."

The internecine battle became bitter. One anti-Musteite stole the roller of the mimeograph machine so that the Muste wing of the faculty couldn't for a time produce manifestoes. The rawness of the emotions on both sides was further exacerbated, Muste feels, "because Brookwood was a pretty closely knit community, where the lives of faculty members and their families and the students had been intimately bound together. It was not only a church, or school, or union, that was being torn while the individuals involved lived in different communities and had family refuges. This time the community itself was disintegrating."

Muste, who had not before become caustic in debate, wounded some of the opposition during one Brookwood faculty meeting when he pointedly quoted George Bernard Shaw's dictum that "those who can, do; those who can't, teach." Toward the end of that bleak winter, Muste became openly shaken by the bickering. "At the meetings," says one combat veteran, "he'd waggle his long finger, his voice would tremble, and that evenness of temperament we'd all thought was an unchangeable characteristic of A.J. was gone."

A February, 1933, statement by the Muste faction to the Brookwood faculty and students reflects the strain in relationships: "We accuse the majority of the Brookwood faculty with lack of that understanding and sympathy and consideration indispensable in such a crisis as the present for the director whom they were only too glad to follow in a period when pay checks were regular. We contend that the heart must have been taken out of the director as to money-raising activities when it seemed so plain that a considerable number of the Brookwood faculty were primarily concerned with protecting their own safe nest at Brookwood, were thrown into a panic when for a period pay checks were held up, were jealous of money raised for the maintenance of activities mainly of Brookwood graduates in the field, were jealous even of money raised by the director and the extension director for the relief of starving miners and their families in West Virginia."

Compromise plans proved unworkable, and the next month, Muste, two other faculty members, and nineteen of the twenty-eight students left Brookwood. "It was a devastating experience," says Helen Norton Starr, "as much for those of us who remained as for A.J. We all had too much affection and respect for him to enjoy having won the fight. The school never had a director after A.J. who had his personal backing and his capacities. It finally closed some three years later."

"Leaving Brookwood," Muste says, "was exceptionally painful for me. For twelve years, we'd lived as part of a very close, warm community. At first, my older children, Nancy and Connie, were desolated by the break. My wife, as usual, did not complain."

"I still think his leaving was a mistake," Mark Starr insists. "As it was, many Brookwood graduates did become useful members of the labor movement, and even now are in executive positions in various unions. But if Brookwood had continued as a center of progressive labor education and had kept lines open to the official

labor movement, the school could have been an exceptionally valuable training area with the coming of the
CIO and the general growth of the mass labor movement. After the New Deal, we could have placed three
times as many students there as we had before."

A. Philip Randolph, President of the Brotherhood of
Sleeping Car Porters, a Vice-President of the AFL-CIO,
and President of the Negro American Labor Council,
also regrets the passing of the school. "There is nothing
comparable to it today, and yet we need a school like
Brookwood today even more than we did then, particularly if we could find a director with A.J.'s integrity and
idealism."

In retrospect, Muste is not so certain Brookwood
would have flourished even if there had not been the
1933 split. He feels that in the decisive years from 1933
to 1939, "any progressive or militant worker worth his
salt was needed on the job. The minds of labor leaders
were too preoccupied with the daily struggle. There
were also constant internal battles over leadership and
policies in the nascent unions into which Brookwood,
insofar as it retained influences, would inevitably have
been dragged. Besides, even if Brookwood had 'flourished,' I would still have been out of it. To have become
identified with the New Deal, with the CIO top leadership, and presently with support of the war—this
would have been for me the abandonment of my deepest convictions and the collapse of inner integrity. In
this context, my instinct that those who disagreed with
me wished to carry Brookwood in a conservative direction seems to me to be validated. This remains true
although some of my own supporters at the time were
also drawn into the New Deal orbit and into acceptance
or support of the war. Of necessity, *my* 'detour' had to
be to the Left."

8

THE EDUCATION OF A TROTSKYITE

"His Destiny (and in Considerable Measure, His Virtue) Lay in the Fact That He Did Not Achieve Power."

A. J. Muste had told the 1929 Brookwood graduating class that "Brookwood stands on the basis of the class struggle; a school which does not accept the capitalist system." Now that he had left the school, Muste was free to intensify the class struggle wherever he could. His decision particularly pleased his most militant allies in the Conference for Progressive Labor Action. For years they had been pressuring him to devote all his time and enormous energy to applying his interpretation of Marxist-Leninist techniques to the land at large.

Among these colleagues was Louis Budenz, executive secretary of C.P.L.A. and editor of *Labor Age*. To Muste's disappointment, Budenz was to become a Communist and editor of the *Daily Worker,* and later a bitter ex-Communist who testified at a number of Congressional hearings against party members, present and past, with whom he had worked. "In the early 1930's," Norman Thomas recalls, "Budenz was a real agitator and

very effective with crowds. I remember him introducing
A.J. to meetings in those days as the 'American Lenin.' "

Muste, Budenz, and other C.P.L.A. leaders were at
first particularly active—while Muste was still at Brookwood—in setting up organizations of the unemployed.
The C.P.L.A.'s cadres were called Unemployed Leagues,
while the Communist equivalent were the Unemployed
Councils. The Musteite Unemployed Leagues were scat-
tered throughout the country. They agitated for raising
local relief allotments, prevented evictions in some
cases, and occasionally marched on state capitals to increase pressure on local government. John Gates, who
was to become a prominent Communist before leaving
the party a few years ago, was a young Communist organizer in Ohio during the period in which Muste was
especially effective in that state among the native-born
unemployed in the small towns. "Our power," he says,
"was among the foreign-born. But Muste was really an
American radical and his Leagues focused directly on
the specific issues without tying them in with a glorifica-
tion of Russia. I remember him at a huge national convention of the Unemployed Leagues in Columbus,
Ohio, in 1933. He was no more a rabble-rouser then
than he is now, but his sober eloquence could really
hold a crowd. And besides, he was a minister, and that
helped make an impression."

It was after the convention in Columbus, at which a
National Unemployed League was organized, that
Muste went to Toledo where the Auto-Lite strike,
largely under the direction of the C.P.L.A., was breaking out. Other radical labor parties, notably the Trotskyites, were impressed with the work of Muste and his
colleagues in Toledo. James Cannon, head of the
Trotsky movement in America, has always been extremely chary of giving credit to other groups, but he

observed that the Musteites in Toledo, through their Unemployed League, had raised the strike action "to a level of mass picketing and militancy far beyond the bounds ever contemplated by the old line craft union bureaucrats."

After Toledo, Muste traveled to central and southern Illinois to report on the strike. Early one morning, Muste began to get the uneasy feeling that he was being followed. He and the two young miners with him drove to the outskirts of Belleville, Illinois, near St. Louis, where a metal plant had been struck. The plant was closed, and the only people in sight were two strikers, acting as observers. The five men sat down on the grass, talking. They discussed the local problem for about an hour, increasingly conscious of a police car parked across the road. Three policemen finally walked over, asked for identification, looked at the red C.P.L.A. membership cards carried by Muste and the miners, and arrested the three of them. After a few hours in jail, Muste and his colleagues were told that they were charged with vagrancy, although Muste had train fare back to New York in his pocket, and one of the miners had proof that he owned the new car in which they had been riding. The second charge was violation of the "Treason Statute" of Illinois—conspiracy to "overthrow the State of Illinois by force and violence." Bail for Muste was set at $20,000. For the two less dangerous miners, bail was lowered to $10,000 each.

Following four days in the county jail, most of the bail money was supplied by a local junk dealer, an elderly German who had been a radical in the old country. American Civil Liberties Union lawyers from St. Louis also came to help, and succeeded in having the vagrancy charge dropped. Muste, however, was tried for "treason." The arresting officer admitted that Muste

had not been doing anything illegal at the struck plant
nor had he been disturbing the peace while sitting on
the grass.

"Why did you arrest him?" asked the judge.

"I thought," said the officer finally, "that any preacher
who was traveling around like that so far from his home
must be up to some mischief."

"He may have something there," Muste muttered.

For nearly a year, the treason charge stood, but suddenly and silently, it was dropped. Muste has long been
curious about the man who provided the bail. "All I
could find out was that up to the time he came forward
and offered the bail, he seems to have had no contact
with radical activity over here. He risked more than
money in suddenly appearing out of nowhere with
nearly forty thousand dollars. He got his money back
and then returned to the obscurity of an aged junk
dealer's life."

Toward the end of 1933, Muste and his C.P.L.A. associates began to set up the American Workers Party
which was intended to be a democratically organized
revolutionary party. The C.P.L.A. itself was diminish-
ing in influence among the unions. It had been effective
in several strikes and, by 1932, was active in pointing up
racketeering in the American Federation of Labor. Yet,
as the C.P.L.A. became more involved in revolutionary
politics, trade unionists grew suspicious of it; and soon
after the American Workers Party was established, it
absorbed the Conference for Progressive Labor Action.
Assessing the C.P.L.A.'s contribution, Joseph Rayback,
in *A History of American Labor* (Macmillan), notes that
the C.P.L.A. did help "revive the idea of industrial
unionism and sparked a movement toward solution of
labor problems through legislative action. By 1932 the
C.P.L.A.'s political program had become the common

property of a large share of labor." At least that part of
its political program which was nonrevolutionary.

The founding of the American Workers Party by
Muste intrigued the Trotskyites. They had finally
stopped trying to fight their way back into the Communist Party, from which they had been expelled in
1928, and had formed the Communist League of America. With considerable brilliance, the Trotskyites had
led teamster strikes in Minneapolis in May and in the
summer of 1934. Now they wanted to widen their base.

Accordingly, in 1934, the Communist League of
America suggested a merger with Muste's American
Workers Party. James Cannon, leader of the Trotskyites, had ambivalent feelings about Muste, but he was
impressed by him. "He was an able and energetic man,"
Cannon wrote in *The History of American Trotskyism*
(Pioneer Publishers), "obviously sincere and devoted
to the cause. . . . His handicap was his background.
Muste had started out in life as a preacher. . . . I have
seen it tried many times, but never successfully. Muste
was, you may say, the last chance and the best chance;
and even he, the best prospect of all, couldn't come
through in the end because of that terrible background
of the church, which had marred him in his formative
years. . . . But despite the handicap of this background,
Muste gave promise because of his exceptional personal
qualities, and because of the great influence he had over
the people associated with him."

In 1960, Cannon, now living in Los Angeles, repeated
his belief that "A.J. was pretty good for a preacher. He
doesn't run with the pack as the others do, no matter
how piously they talk. And in those years, in the rough
and rowdy world of militant strikers, impatient unemployed demonstrators and godless revolutionaries, he
was accepted and respected on all sides. Yet Muste

always remained a man apart. There was a slight aura of godliness about him. All the others were on a first name or nickname basis. But Muste was always 'A.J.' I never heard him called anything else and don't know for sure to this day what his first name is, if he has one. I remember during one heated discussion in a factional fight, a young comrade began to swear and denounced a statement by another speaker as a damned lie. Then, remembering where he was, he checked himself, and added: 'If the women comrades present and comrade Muste will excuse me.' "

Cannon had visited Trotsky in southern France and asked his advice about merging with the Musteites. "Trotsky," Cannon recalls, "was fully in favor of it, and he was also greatly interested in the personality of Muste. He entertained some hopes that Muste would develop into a real Bolshevik later. During the entire period of our association with Muste, Trotsky's attitude toward him was very respectful and friendly. When we got into a serious dispute with Muste later, Trotsky specifically cautioned me in a personal letter to keep the dispute within fraternal limits and to be careful not to say or do anything that would strike at Muste's prestige."

In dealing with the American Workers Party, Cannon observed that while Muste was not the only leader of the A.W.P., "he was the one in the middle, the moderator, the central leader who balanced everything between the contending sides." The merger was accomplished in December, 1934, and the new organization was named the Workers Party of the United States. *The Militant,* the Trotskyites' paper, reported triumphantly: "New party launched into its tremendous undertaking: The overthrow of capitalist rule in America and the creation of a workers' state."

The Communists were infuriated. The *Daily Worker* warned the Musteites against "the trap of counter-revolutionary Trotskyism" and warned the Trotskyites against "unity with Muste, the champion of bourgeois nationalism." They were to be particularly incensed the next year when the first broadcast of the "Town Meeting of the Air" scheduled a forum on "Which Way America—Fascism, Communism, Socialism or Democracy?" Lawrence Dennis represented the Fascists, Norman Thomas the Socialists, and Raymond Moley the forces of political democracy. Muste, a staunch Trotskyite by then, was chosen to give the Communist point of view, and the American Stalinists complained bitterly.

During the broadcast, Muste, however, had been explicit in disassociating himself from the Stalinists. "I'm not representing the Communist Party," he began his statement, "or the Third International, with which I have no connection. I'm setting forth the historical position of Communism as it applies to the experience of the modern working class."

The collaboration between Muste and the Trotskyites soon became turbulent. Muste had not been sufficiently aware of the implications of a change in tactics that Leon Trotsky had dictated to his international followers. Trotsky had first instructed his party members in France to work their way into the Socialist French Left. In September, 1934, the Trotskyites there dutifully executed what came to be known as the "French turn" by joining the Socialist Party of France as a faction which would bore from within.

Muste did know about the "French turn," but he had been assured by Cannon before the merger that the tactic was only to be applied in France. Cannon was not entirely candid with Muste at the time; but as Cannon has said, "A Trotskyite will do anything for his

party, even if he has to crawl on his belly in the mud."
Cannon also placed party discipline over personal
friendship, a rule he tried unsuccessfully to teach
Muste. Cannon once complained that Muste protected
his friends in the movement. "That is one of the gravest
offenses against the revolutionary party," Cannon asserted. "Friendship, which is a very good thing in personal life, must always be subordinated to principles
and the interests of the movement. But Muste wouldn't
listen."

"A.J.," Mark Starr has observed, "wasn't built for the
kind of expediency in personal relationships and the
infighting at which the Trotskyites were so expert."
Cannon finally agreed. "Muste," he said, "is too much
of a gentleman."

Muste did take Cannon at his word that the American
Trotskyites were not planning their own "French turn."
By 1935, however, Cannon and his lieutenants proposed
that the Workers Party of the United States join the
larger Socialist Party with the aim of eventually taking
it over. Muste was appalled, and fought the "turn." He
was convinced the move would seriously compromise
the integrity of the Workers Party in that it violated
working-class ethics.

Muste was right concerning the dubious ethics of the
Trotskyites, as Cannon later confirmed after he had
defeated Muste and affected the merger between the
A.W.P. and the Socialists. In 1937, the Trotskyites were
expelled from the Socialist Party because of their divi-
sive tactics. Cannon remembers telling Trotsky about
the weakened condition in which he and his forces had
left the Socialists: "Comrade Trotsky said that alone
would have justified our entry into the organization
even if we hadn't gained a single new member."

Muste was severely disturbed by his experiences with

the Trotsky methodology. "What might have happened if the pre-merger understanding that we were not proposing a 'French Turn' here had been kept is obviously a matter for speculation," he has observed in *Liberation*. "The deterioration of the American Left in the years since could hardly have been worse than it proved to be, and I am convinced that the kind of infighting and maneuvering which went on in the Workers Party, and which was by no means confined to it, had a good deal to do with that deterioration."

Almost equally troubling to Muste was the defection to the Communist Party of Louis Budenz and several other of his closest associates in the same month, October, 1935, in which he was defeated within his own party by the Trotskyites. It was becoming quite clear to Muste that he had taken a "detour" into revolutionary politics that had not worked. "Yet," he later said, "the ultimate betrayal, the sacrifice of my inner integrity, would have been to stay out of the struggles of the thirties, to have not been on the side of the oppressed. I do not essentially regret the course I took, not that regret would do any good. And I did put the theories of 'lesser evil,' of 'realism,' of the inescapability or necessity of violence, or revolutionary dictatorship, and so on, to the test of experience. I am, therefore, not beguiled by contemporary expressions of them. I am sure my earlier experience has been helpful to me in my attempts to develop nonviolent methods and a more revolutionary pacifist movement in later years. If people tell me that there is no clearly defined nonviolent way to deal with a situation, then I answer that we have got to experiment and find one. God knows we have experimented long enough with other methods."

Dean Walter G. Muelder of Boston University agrees with this appraisal of the benefits of the Trotsky years for Muste's later work: "He used many of the tools of analysis which the dialectical methods of Marxism taught him. Instead of drawing so-called realistic conclusions from this method, he applied it to alleged realism and found it wanting."

"Nonetheless," says Sidney Lens, a labor leader and historian who has been associated with Muste in various projects for nearly thirty years, "that particular detour he took was a very bad mistake. Muste, more than any other left-wing leader in that period, had the personal force and the intellectual capacity to build a native American radical movement. He lost that chance by becoming involved with the Trotskyites."

Though disillusioned, Muste continued to work in the labor movement as a Trotskyite until the summer of 1936. In the spring of that year, he took part in the Goodyear Rubber strike in Akron, one of the first applications by American labor of the sit-in technique then also being tried in France. The tactic, largely suggested at Akron by Muste, was later used on a larger scale by the auto workers in Detroit and Flint.

As absorbing as strike activity remained, Muste had become emotionally and physically exhausted. When several friends collected funds to send him and his wife to Europe for a vacation, he agreed to go. "The collection," Milton Mayer observed, "overflowed with contributions from people who hated Musteism and loved Muste."

The trip was not entirely for pleasure. Muste was part of a delegation attending an international meeting of Trotskyites in Paris, and he also accepted an invitation to visit Trotsky himself. "When I sailed out of New York harbor on a June day," Muste wrote a few years later, "I had not the faintest idea that I should return with my basic outlook and convictions changed and that my first act on returning in August would be to sever my relations with the Trotskyist movement."

"His friends," Milton Mayer reported, "saw him—the class warrior—for the last time as the boat pulled out from Hoboken pier with his skinny arm raised in the clenched-fist salute of bloody revolution."

Trotsky was then living in Norway in a small town near Oslo. Muste and the embattled revolutionary enjoyed their week of discussions. "I found him very human," says Muste. "He had a very attractive, vital personality. Although he was certainly autocratic in dealing with his followers, he was not with me. I was much impressed at his intellectual versatility. He talked of literature and philosophy as well as politics with much knowledge and insight. He did, it seemed to me, lack a sense of humor, although there was no lack of sarcasm. It was also clear that he was quite out of touch with the realities of the workers' movement in America.

"Although my faction had lost in the battle of the 'French turn,'" Muste continues, "Trotsky seemed anxious to have me stay within the party. 'Perhaps,' Trotsky said rather surprisingly at the end of our talk, 'an American version of the "French turn" was not the right tactic, but it *has* been done, and you should not let it drive you out of the party. You have too much to give.' We parted amicably, but I would not commit myself definitely to remain within the party."

Nearly twenty years later, Muste met Isaac Deutscher, a biographer of Trotsky, in London. Deutscher had been permitted by Trotsky's widow to examine much of the Trotsky correspondence that had not yet been made publicly available. "You're quite unusual as a figure in Trotsky's correspondence," Deutscher told Muste. "You're one of the very few people to whom Trotsky always referred with respect and affection." "I

suppose the reason," Muste speculates, "was that
Trotsky admired people who could organize and who
had rapport with masses of people. He knew that our
American Workers Party had achieved contact with
large groups of workers and that where we had operated the Stalinists had not been able to get a foothold."

Muste feels "there was an element of charm, gentleness and softness (in the better sense of the term) in
Trotsky that was apparently totally lacking in his great
antagonist; but, as is often the case, this did not exclude
a capacity for ruthlessness and for glorying in that capacity. His destiny (and in considerable measure, his
virtue) lay in the fact that he did not achieve power."

As Muste traveled through Europe that summer, he
became more and more depressed at the "maneuvers of
bombing planes and the marching soldiers everywhere."
The year itself, 1936, was a turning point. Events in
Russia indicated the further calcification of the dictatorship. The Spanish Civil War was clearly going to lead
to violence throughout Europe. The Germans were
building their air force, and the British Labour Party
had ended its opposition to disarmament.

"Moreover," Muste remembers, "I was convinced before that summer was over that the labor and revolutionary movement had in so many places suffered
defeat, and in others had come to an impasse, largely because of ethical and spiritual shortcomings. The idealism and *élan* seemed to have largely gone out of the
revolutionary movement in Europe. Factionalism and
lack of confidence by the membership in the leadership
and in each other had been eating at its vitals."

9

THE RETURN
TO NONVIOLENCE
AND THE F.O.R.

"Revolutionists Cannot Be Solitary."

TOWARD THE end of July, 1936, the Mustes were sight-seeing in Paris. While walking along the streets of the Left Bank, they passed the old, dourly massive church of St. Sulpice. The Mustes went inside. "St. Sulpice seemed very much cluttered with statues," Muste has recalled. "In addition, repair work was going on and there was a good deal of scaffolding, especially near the altar. Yet somehow, almost from the moment I came into the sanctuary, a deep and what I can only describe as a singing peace came over me. I don't mean that this peace took the place of turbulence. I had all along acted pretty conscientiously according to my lights and was not aware of any inner conflict. But that afternoon, I did have a sense of comfortable though not exuberant physical well-being. Yet the sudden *new* sensation was one of a deepened, a fathomless peace, and of the spirit hearing what I suppose people are trying to describe when they use the stuffy and banal phrase, 'the music of the spheres.' The Bible has worthier words when it speaks of the time 'when the morning stars sang together.' I seated myself on a bench and looked toward the altar and the cross. I felt, 'This is where you belong, in the church, not outside it.' "

Muste was not yet thinking about returning to the ministry, but he was anxious to reestablish the connection between his Christian pacifist background and his political activities. The experience at St. Sulpice also made him realize that there had been a relationship between his Marxist faith and the Calvinism of his early years. "The noblest participants in the revolutionary movement, it occurred to me, are inspired by the faith that 'historic forces make the triumph of socialism inevitable.' But a force which makes for an invincible world of righteousness to which the individual must surrender himself utterly was also a pretty fair definition of God, and of a Calvinist God."

Having returned to Christianity, Muste remained a Socialist. In fact, he was what could be termed a Calvinist Socialist. Three years after his reconversion at St. Sulpice, Muste wrote in the magazine, *Christendom:* ". . . the salvation which God in Christ brings I have never been able to think of as 'individual,' in the sense of 'not social.' For one thing, in its most intimate, personal form, it is an experience of the abasement of the self before God, in which a man knows—knows with his whole being, 'existentially'—that he is the murderer, the thief, the ingrate, the lustful one. Thus he becomes one with his fellows. Perhaps no one has ever expressed the attitude which flowers from such experience more clearly than Gene Debs in his speech before being sentenced to Atlanta during World War I: 'While there is a lower class, I am in it; while there is a criminal element, I am of it; while there is a soul in prison, I am not free.' "

For five weeks, none of his friends in America heard

from Muste. Then Cara Cook, with whom he had worked closely at Brookwood and with whom he had remained in contact, received a postcard telling her when he and his wife would land. Shortly afterward, she was startled by a sixteen-page, single-spaced letter from Muste in which he announced his break with Trotskyism and his return to religion. "I was thunder-struck," Miss Cook remembers, "especially after his enthusiastic letters about the meetings with Trotsky. Then, all of a sudden, this—this document came. It turned the world upside down."

"War," the letter began, "is the central problem for us all today." Muste went on to insist that the labor movements, the Socialists and the Communists could no longer be relied on to prevent war. Nor would even a "genuine" Marxist-Leninist movement, in contrast to the grotesque mutation in the U.S.S.R., succeed in hold-ing off war. Nor was there hope of the proletariat's recognizing the necessity of Socialism and peace with-out fundamental changes in basic human attitudes. "We are thrust back," Muste wrote, "upon the problems of human behavior" that underlie and often twist any sys-tem out of direction. Morality, he continued, is the basic dynamic for durable social change. "International war and coercion at home will continue to exist for just so long as people regard these things as suitable, as even conceivable, instruments of policy."

Muste was again advocating Christian nonviolence, but an active nonviolence that would be combined with elements of Marxism in order to change society. He was still a revolutionary. "The Christian position does not mean to justify or condone the capitalist system. Quite the contrary. It provides the one measure by which the capitalist system stands thoroughly and effectively con-demned. It stands condemned because it makes the

Christian relation in its full sense, the relation of brotherhood between human beings, impossible. The domination of the acquisitive motive under capitalism, the fact that each must . . . seek to outwit and overcome the other . . . makes love in the full sense impossible. . . . So long, however, as the matter remains on the plane of economics and self-interest, no one is in a position to condemn another. When we feel indignation, as we do even in spite of ourselves, we then enter the realm of standards and values, the realm in which moral judgment is pronounced, the realm in which ethical and spiritual appeals are made . . . the realm of morality and religion."

His next step, Muste said in ending the letter, was to find a place for himself in a Christian movement and begin to make over that movement and the world from that base. "Revolutionists cannot be solitary, cannot form a revolutionary movement *ab novo*."

The news of Muste's split with the Trotskyites circulated rapidly through the radical movement. Word came to the Trotskyite comrades in Minneapolis who two years before had cheered Muste and had even bought him a new suit. Comrade Vincent Dunne read the news in a letter one morning, and turned to a fellow worker, Bill Brown. "Bill, what do you think? Muste's gone back to the church."

"Well, I'll be damned," said Bill Brown. There was a mournful silence. "Say, Vincent," Brown turned to him indignantly. "We ought to get that suit back."

Muste's first job as an ex-Trotskyite was with the Fellowship of Reconciliation, which he had originally joined in 1916. He had been national chairman of the F.O.R. from 1926-29, but as he became more involved with revolutionary labor action, he had allowed his membership to become inactive. On his return from

Europe in August, 1936, the first public meeting Muste attended was the annual conference of the F.O.R. He told of his return to pacifism, and somewhat apprehensively, he waited for the reaction of these long-term pacifists who had not felt the need to try a detour.

"They immediately elected me to the national council of the F.O.R.," says Muste. "It was a fairly courageous act for them." "Not so courageous," according to John Nevin Sayre, who was then co-chairman of the F.O.R. "Nor at all surprising. We knew that A.J.'s pacifism had worn pretty thin in the preceding years, but he had never let his personal relations with any of us become corroded. We knew the man he was, and we had no hesitation in inviting him back."

The Fellowship of Reconciliation, with which Muste has since become closely identified, was conceived in 1914 by Friedrich Siegmund-Schultze, pacifist chaplain to the Kaiser, and Henry Hodgkin, an English Quaker. On August 2 of that year, the day before war was declared, the two men had shaken hands in a Cologne railroad station and had pledged to keep "the bonds of Christian love unbroken across the frontier." The F.O.R. came into formal existence toward the end of 1914 at Trinity College, Cambridge, with 128 British members. Hodgkin, its chairman, came to America less than a year later. In a meeting at Garden City, Long Island, attended by sixty-eight pacifists, he presided at the founding of the American F.O.R. Since then, the F.O.R.'s main activities have been against war and for international understanding. Its humanist principles, however, have also been consistently applied to other problems requiring reconciliation.

The general policy of the F.O.R. has been to organize or help form groups dealing with specific problems and then to withdraw to other work when the new organizations become self-sufficient. Among the groups that have received an initial impetus from the F.O.R. or F.O.R. members have been the American Civil Liberties Union, the National Conference of Christians and Jews, the Workers Defense League, the Congress of Racial Equality, the Church Peace Mission, the Society for Social Responsibility in Science, and the American Committee on Africa.

The Fellowship's credo is flexible enough so that it has always contained members of widely varying background and views, including ministers of various denominations. American membership is currently 13,000, and there are some 28,000 additional F.O.R. members in twenty-five countries. The F.O.R.'s Statement of Purpose declares that its members, although they "do not bind themselves to any exact form of words . . . strive to build a social order which will suffer no individual or group to be exploited for the profit or pleasure of another, and which will assure to all the means for realizing the best possibilities of life. . . . It is intended that members shall work out these purposes in their own ways. There is no uniform program of social reconstruction to which all are committed."

During both world wars, the F.O.R. helped conscientious objectors, in and out of prison. Its magazine, then called *The World Tomorrow,* started printing articles about Gandhi's use of nonviolence in the 1920's, and, in the early 1940's, the Fellowship started to apply nonviolent, direct-action techniques at home in the desegregation of restaurants and other public facilities. It has since conducted many interracial workshops in nonviolence. In contrast to several other liberal, Northern-based organizations, F.O.R. chapters and meetings in the South have always been integrated.

The F.O.R. has also been involved in labor relations.

Muste, for example, was an active member of the Fellowship when he became a leader in the 1919 Lawrence strike. Other F.O.R. staff workers and general members have been effective in mediating strikes and organizing relief for strikers, and the influence of F.O.R. members has been credited on occasion by local police with having prevented violence on the picket lines.

When A. J. Muste returned to the F.O.R. staff in 1936, it was as Industrial Secretary. His assignment was to increase the effectiveness of nonviolent techniques in industrial disputes. In the winter of 1936-37, Muste participated in a hosiery workers' strike in Reading, Pennsylvania. Among the young leadership of the union were both Socialists and F.O.R. members. The strike was long and bitter. At its climax, some twenty of the workers, including several young ladies, twice stretched out in the middle of a road so that trucks on the way to the mill could not pass. "The technique was effective," says Muste. "It not only encouraged the other workers to avoid violent retaliation, but, as a result of the nonviolent climate we helped create, there were practically no more physical clashes during the rest of the strike, in contrast to what was happening elsewhere at the time. The police roughed up a few workers, but gradually they too became affected by the 'soul force' of the strikers. It takes time for nonviolent techniques to work on the opposition, but almost invariably, a marked change in attitude does occur on both sides over a considerable period of time.

"I've seen the same process of change," Muste continues, "in the New York civil defense protests. In 1955, the first time we refused to take shelter, the police were aggressively hostile. In succeeding years, as we continued to act nonviolently, the police became increasingly courteous; and in our last attempts in 1960 and 1961, the authorities made no real effort to break up the demonstrations."

Muste continued to try to reconcile labor disputes until August, 1937, when he became director of the Presbyterian Labor Temple on Fourteenth Street and Second Avenue in New York. The Temple, which has since changed in nature, was established in 1910 by Charles Stelzle, a Presbyterian minister. At that time, the lower East Side still contained sweatshops, and the neighborhood was a slum. Stelzle had been brought up there, had been active in the machinists' union before studying for the ministry, and it had been his idea to make the neighborhood church a place where Christianity could be interpreted to working people. The staff of the Temple was assigned, furthermore, to interpret the working people to other churches. There were open forums, guest lectures, and study classes. Labor unions held their meetings in the church; there was room for the homeless to sleep; and, in time, the Temple became a uniquely venturesome center for adult education. In 1918-20, for example, Will Durant gave a series of lectures at the church which later became *The Story of Philosophy.*

The Labor Temple was clearly the right context for a man of Muste's background and enthusiasms. Although its director was not absolutely required to be an ordained minister, it helped if he were, since there was a small congregation to care for as well as the open forums and classes. Muste was still technically ordained, although he had wandered far from the pulpit since the Lawrence strike. He had remained on the rolls of the Suffolk West Association of the Congregational Church of Massachusetts after leaving the Newtonville pastorate during the First World War. The Presbytery of New York was willing to accept a letter of credentials affirming Muste's status as a minister from the Suffolk West Association, and Muste was once more in the church.

Muste devoted about a third of his time at the Temple to preparing sermons and serving the needs of his parishioners. For the rest, he lectured in other churches, organized the adult education classes, and presided over the frequently turbulent forums and debates on Wednesday and Sunday nights. The stormiest encounter was an evening with Eugene Lyons, who had become thoroughly disillusioned with the Soviet Union, and Moissaye J. Olgin, a fervent Communist. Nearly nine hundred partisans on both sides jammed the Temple that night, and police were stationed on the street in anticipation of violence. Muste recalls that the audience was about equally divided in its sentiments, but Lyons, who can still hear the whistling squads, believes the odds against him were much greater.

As soon as Lyons began to speak, there was an uproar from the pro-Soviet faction. "I didn't come down here to talk to nincompoops," Lyons shouted back, and the audience exploded into a roaring mass. Muste tried to restore order, and somehow made himself audible after much difficulty. The preacher stood in the center of the stage, and said with his customary implacable reasonableness, "This church has been on this corner for nearly thirty years. It does not believe in what at least half of you stand for, but it does insist—and always has —that absolute freedom of political discussion must be allowed inside its walls. I intend to continue that tradition."

There was a sudden shout from the crowd, different in character from the angry howling before. Muste was applauded lustily, and returned somewhat stunned, to his seat. "I hadn't really expected to get them under control," he says, "but both sides became swept up in an emotional support of free speech. Lyons was able to continue, and although there was a long, rough question period with frequent bursts of whistling, there was no violence."

In 1940, Muste left the Labor Temple to return to the F.O.R. as Executive Secretary. He was the chief designer of policy and administrative head of the American branch of the Fellowship. Although he remained a skillful reconciler, Muste was always identified with the more radical section of the Fellowship, particularly with regard to the initiation of nonviolent direct-action projects. "Some of the more conservative F.O.R. members and executives," says a current F.O.R. official, "occasionally found A.J.'s ideas pretty hard to swallow; but because of the nature of his own nonarrogant personality, there was never an open break. He was so respected personally that his opponents in the F.O.R. didn't dare kick him out, although a few members of the National Council must have been sorely tempted at times."

Although Muste has been considerably more active in direct-action demonstrations since becoming Secretary Emeritus of the F.O.R. in 1953, he did not allow his penchant for reconciliation to limit those of his direct-action projects which were most important to him during his term as F.O.R. Executive Secretary. James Bristol of the American Friends Service Committee remembers that about 1946, "A.J. cancelled an F.O.R. trip to the West Coast in order to take part in a vigil and direct-action demonstration at the Pentagon. He was severely criticized by some F.O.R. members, and even by quite responsible F.O.R. people, because the cancellation was made pretty much at the last minute. A.J. pointed out that through the years he had kept engagements, and that he would continue to keep them, but his Good Friday Vigil was such an important matter that he felt impelled to give up the other plans in its favor." And Muste did go to Washington.

"It is true," says Muste, "there were those in the F.O.R. who thought several of us were overemphasizing that kind of activity, but essentially, I was not constricted. Besides, the F.O.R. council made a remarkable decision after the Second War which allowed all members of the staff to act according to their convictions provided they made it clear that they were not demonstrating in the name of the F.O.R. in such activities as tax refusal and advising youngsters not to register for the draft. There was also a general understanding that outside involvement could not lead to serious neglect of F.O.R. duties."

Muste, because of the prodigious enthusiasm and stamina which have characterized him all his life, was continually able to find time for multiple outside involvements while taking full care of his F.O.R. obligations. He also devoted much energy to finding and training protégés within the Fellowship of Reconciliation.

10

THE
DISCIPLES

*"He Certainly Can Make His Influence
Felt Without Giving Direct Orders."*

DURING HIS years as executive secretary of the Fellowship of Reconciliation, A. J. Muste kept a rather loose
rein on his staff. He was very careful in recruitment,
but once he believed in a staff member's integrity and
initiative, Muste allowed him considerable freedom.
Several of the Musteites in the F.O.R. have been responsible in the past two decades for significant work in
race relations, peace education, and African affairs.

James Farmer, for example, is currently national director of the Congress of Racial Equality after having
served as program director of the National Association
for the Advancement of Colored People. In February,
1942, Farmer, then race relations secretary of the
F.O.R., made the initial proposal to the F.O.R. which
led to the creation of C.O.R.E. Farmer recommended
the formation of a group (composed of both pacifists
and nonpacifists) which would commit itself to nonviolent action against discrimination. In April of that
year, Farmer was authorized by the National Council of

the F.O.R. to spend some of his time on the project. That authorization was spurred by the enthusiasm of A. J. Muste.

Farmer then became one of the founders in Chicago of the first C.O.R.E. chapter. Among the other Muste-ites who helped strengthen the organization during the following years were Bayard Rustin and George Houser. For most of the 1940's, the unpaid Executive Director of C.O.R.E. was Houser, whose official work in those years was on the staff of the Fellowship. Rustin, who was youth secretary of the F.O.R. when C.O.R.E. was formed, had already started one-man applications of nonviolent techniques against racial discrimination, and his descriptions of his experiences during national lecture tours helped create a climate for the support of the Congress of Racial Equality.

Houser and Rustin, moreover, organized the first "freedom ride" as far back as 1947. Its name then was "the journey of reconciliation," and it was cosponsored by the Fellowship of Reconciliation and C.O.R.E. In the preceding year, the Supreme Court had issued its first decision banning segregation in interstate travel. To test the effectiveness of that decision, Houser and Rustin formed the first interracial team to travel through the South (the upper South) in a confrontation of prejudice by nonviolence.

There were arrests, and Rustin, among others, served thirty days on a North Carolina chain gang. There was only one incident of violence, however, and as James Peck, a member of the team, has pointed out, the "jour-ney of reconciliation" did prove that at least some bus drivers and passengers were ready to accept desegrega-tion. In his book, *Freedom Ride* (Simon and Schuster), Peck noted: "Aboard buses where drivers ignored our Negroes sitting in front seats, passengers did likewise. . . .

We realized that our journey had not prompted Negroes to flock immediately to front seats on Southern buses. But we hoped that a few Southern Negroes would act as a result of the example we had set and that the desegregation process would thus get slowly under way. A number of students and a few adults whom we had encountered in the course of our meetings had pledged to sit unsegregated on their next trip back home or visiting relatives. In the light of our hope, it was gratifying fourteen years later when I observed on the Freedom Ride that Negroes occupied front seats without hesitation, and drivers did not give them dirty looks in scanning the buses before departure."

A. J. Muste's influence—direct and indirect—on the nonviolent movement in the South has continued through the years. The Reverend James Lawson, for instance, has indicated unusual qualities of leadership, and there is some speculation that he may eventually eclipse Martin Luther King. Lawson, who had worked for the F.O.R., was one of the organizers of the 1960 Nashville sit-ins. As a result, he was expelled from the Vanderbilt University Divinity School and precipitated a crisis of conscience among many Vanderbilt faculty members. Lawson credits Muste with having been among the first to awaken his interest in nonviolence. Like Martin Luther King, Lawson first heard and was impressed by Muste when the then F.O.R. executive secretary appeared at his school as a guest lecturer. "He handled a violent heckler easily and gently," Lawson recalls, "and besides, he made excellent sense."

George Houser, now executive secretary of the American Committee on Africa, has described the atmosphere at the F.O.R. during Muste's administration. "One reason," Houser explains, "A.J. was able to maintain equilibrium in the F.O.R. between us and the

Anna Huizenga, the future Mrs. Muste, in front of her family's home in Rock Valley, Iowa, 1906.

A. J. Muste while minister of the Fort Washington Collegiate Church, New York (1909-14).

Nancy and Connie Muste at Brookwood, ca. *1921*.

At Brookwood in the late 1920's: Mrs. Muste, John Muste, A. J. Muste, and E. J. Lever, an early graduate of Brookwood, later active in the steelworkers' union.

At Brookwood in the 1920's, from left to right: David Saposs, labor historian; Arthur W. Calhoun, sociologist; Mildred Calhoun; Josephine Colby, teacher of English and one of the founders of the American Federation of Teachers; A. J. Muste.

The Muste children—Connie, Nancy, and John—at Brookwood in the late 1920's.

A. J. Muste while Executive Secretary of the Fellowship of Reconciliation, in the 1940's.

Lincoln W. Barnes, The Photo Shop, Amherst, Mass.

Anna Muste, in the late 1940's.

Sarony, Incorporated, New York

A. J. Muste, Secretary Emeritus of the American Fellowship of Reconciliation, with Muriel Lester, retiring Traveling Secretary of the International F.O.R. and John Nevin Sayre, Chairman of the International F.O.R. (1954).

A. J. Muste, F.O.R. Secretary Emeritus, en route to France, Germany, and U.S.S.R., addresses a crowd of 3,300 marchers and 2,500 others at Trafalgar Square rally in London. Canon Collins, chairman of the rally, is at the right. The demonstration was against H-bombs and in support of the crew of the **Golden Rule** *(June 22, 1958).*

Austin Underwood.

A. J. Muste, January, 1956.

Omaha Action, summer of 1959.

> *A. J. Muste approaching the gate of the Mead, Nebraska, missile base, followed by Ross Anderson and Karl Meyer. Muste is addressing an Air Force officer who had ordered him not to enter.*

Ross Anderson, A. J. Muste, and Karl Meyer being ushered out of the Mead missile base after their first entry.

more conservative members was his complete refusal to
indulge in any of the petty politics you sometimes find
even—in fact, especially—in high-minded organizations.
I was once looking through the files, and I found a note
to A.J. from an important F.O.R. official who didn't
believe I should have been brought onto the national
staff because he felt I was unsuited to the work. Muste
had never mentioned this to me or anyone else. I asked
him about it, and all he said was, 'You're here, aren't
you?' There was nothing else to talk about. Under most
administrators, incidents like this are magnified and can
lead to long, internecine battles."

"For those thirteen years," says another former Fellowship of Reconciliation field secretary, "A.J. *was* the
F.O.R. At the staff meetings, he seldom said anything
until the rest of us had finished. Then he formulated
his own position from what he considered had been the
most astute points we had made." John Nevin Sayre,
who was co-secretary of the F.O.R. with Muste for some
time and is now active in the work of the International
F.O.R., was and is more conservative than Muste. Sayre
usually led the opposition. He recalls that "Not only
would A.J. usually speak last in a meeting, but 90 percent of the time, he'd swing everybody else his way
when he did speak."

Muste also brought more wit to F.O.R. deliberations
than had been customary. John Oliver Nelson of the
Yale Divinity School, a former national chairman of
the Fellowship, observes that "the annual meetings of
the National Council dealt with important matters but
were, I'm afraid, rather dull until it was A.J.'s turn at
the end. He would rise, and, as usual, he'd have a folded
copy of *The New York Times* in his hand. A sort of
precursor of Mort Sahl, he'd analyze the news in a way
that was both provocative and droll. He's one of the

very few full-time peace workers I've known who is so
often mischievous."

A former F.O.R. worker recalls having been awed in
the late 1940's at being allowed to attend for the first
time a luncheon of the Fellowship's hierarchy. "A. J.
Muste walked in. I thought of his past revolutionary
activities and his consistent courage in working for
peace. I was waiting eagerly for his first word. A.J.
looked around, and asked, 'How did the Dodgers make
out yesterday?' I was shocked."

The serious young man had been almost as appalled
at noting that Muste smoked fairly constantly at the
luncheon. Muste's daughter, Connie, who worked for
the F.O.R. for a time, points out that "among religious
people, there are some who frown on smoking, and the
subject occasionally came up in the F.O.R. office where
opinion among the staff was divided. Once, at the noon
meeting (the whole office force met for a few minutes at
noon for announcements and a brief meditation) my
father read with great glee the pronouncement of some
psychologist to the effect that there were indeed deep
psychological reasons why people smoked, but that there
were also deep psychological reasons why some people
were against smoking."

On another occasion, a prominent F.O.R. member
and financial supporter wrote Muste complaining that
one of his field workers had been seen drinking beer
with some of the young people in her local church. As a
result, she concluded, she was not going to send further
contributions to the Fellowship. The lady also owned a
business and was fighting all attempts to unionize her
workers. Muste replied to her indignant charges by saying that although he would not necessarily defend a field
worker who mixed beer with work, he did not know

the exact circumstances of the incident, and so could
not yet comment. He would, he added, make an adverse
judgment, however, on someone who exploited employees. The next year, the woman exceeded all her
previous contributions to the Fellowship, and in time
she even recognized the union.

Muste gave advice on personal as well as organizational problems to the young people he kept bringing
into the Fellowship, and to others he met on his ex-
tensive lecture tours. Bayard Rustin, who has continued
to do important organizational work in various desegregation and disarmament campaigns in recent years, first
met Muste in 1940. Rustin was then a student at the
City College of New York and a member of the Young
Communist League. Raised as a Quaker, Rustin had
become increasingly troubled by moral problems involved in working within the tight Communist discipline. He was looking for counsel, and turned to Muste.
As has happened with several people who later have
become strongly influenced by Muste, Rustin's first
impression of the quiet radical was not especially favor-
able. Muste listened much more than he talked and
seemed to lack the fire for which Rustin was looking.

When Russia was invaded by Germany and the "im-
perialist war" instantly became a "people's war," Rustin's dilemma intensified. "I had to talk with someone
or go mad," he recalls. Rustin called on Muste again.
"This time, I was deeply impressed. Muste was as
oriented in Marxism as the Communists I knew. He
wasn't at all the fuzzy 'liberal' pacifist type I'd expected.
He didn't try to proselytize me, although he did explain
several of the principles of nonviolent direct action. At
the end of our talk, he said simply that if I examined all
the possible positions I could take and measured them
against my background and experiences, I'd come to

the right decision. Soon after, I joined the staff of the
Fellowship of Reconciliation."

Rustin became a close associate of Muste. "He was so
productive a leader because he was so realistic. What
some have called his saintliness is combined with unusual political shrewdness. He also knows and admits
enough of the existence of evil not to share the easy
optimism of the average pacifist. In my own case, I
learned more about nonviolence from him than in all
my subsequent reading. I finally recognized that the
pacifism by personal example of my Quaker youth was
not enough. The social institutions—as well as man himself—had to be changed. Muste never made the mistake
that many other pacifists have made. He didn't believe
that lobbying and writing letters can be effective just
by themselves. You have to act, and act with your body,
in nonviolent demonstrations to create social dislocation. I carried over his lessons to my later work with
Martin Luther King.

"In addition," Rustin continues, "Muste himself has
always been willing to go to jail for his principles, and
those principles are remarkably consistent. He is
strongly anti-Communist but believes in complete freedom of argument. During the worst of the McCarthy
period, A.J. suggested that the F.O.R. sponsor a Paul
Robeson concert, since Robeson was having so much
trouble finding a place to be heard. A.J.'s idea was
turned down, but only after a big fight. Similarly, A.J.
was one of the relatively few churchmen who publicly
protested the executions of Julius and Ethel Rosenberg
—an issue on which many liberals were reluctant to be
counted—and he circulated petitions for clemency."

Another F.O.R. alumnus who first met Muste at a
time of personal crisis was George Houser. In October,
1940, Houser was one of nine students at the Union

Theological School who refused to register for the draft. "There was tremendous pressure from the board of trustees to expel us," says Houser. "The seminary refused, but several faculty members tried very hard to talk us out of our position. Others were mildly for us, but no one gave us the active and outspoken support A.J. did. We contacted him because he himself advocated nonregistration. He gave us considerable advice on strategy, and much moral encouragement. When we went to prison, A.J. kept in touch with us, and in one letter he invited me to join the staff of the F.O.R."

While working in the Fellowship, Houser, with Muste's advice and encouragement, set up several direct-action projects in race relations as well as his work for the Congress of Racial Equality. "During those years of watching A.J.'s methods," Houser says, "I became convinced there wasn't a trace of fanaticism in him. His mind is primarily an analytical one, and there is a calmness in his commitment that allows him to remain cool under exceedingly trying circumstances. He's also somewhat of a fox about getting what he wants done. He's a keen politician. Yet he's no dictator. People like Bayard Rustin, myself, and the other young people he brought into the F.O.R. are not temperamentally given to taking orders with which we don't agree or which are relayed to us in an authoritarian manner. We couldn't have stayed if he had tried to force his views on us. But he certainly can make his influence felt without giving direct orders."

"Another thing about Muste," says civil libertarian Roger Baldwin, who is not enthusiastic about most of Muste's direct-action demonstrations, "is that when he does get out of the office, as he prefers to do, he's not afraid of injuring his reputation or his physical well-being by following through in what he believes. That

way he has always set quite an example to the younger
people in the movement. I do think though that he also
has an actor's sense of always wanting to be part of the
act when the act is sufficiently dramatic. For all his
lack of external flamboyance, I would not say that A.J.
is self-effacing."

A man who, unlike Baldwin, is an ardent direct actionist and has participated in several protest demonstrations against preparations for nuclear warfare in
recent years, agrees that Muste enjoys his role as the
leader of the peace movement in America. The peace
worker adds, "I don't mean that he's egocentric. I think
rather that part of his desire to be always in the vanguard of demonstrations and other activity for peace is
his realization that his skill in reconciling so many different fragments of the peace movement is not enough.
Once policy-making has been democratically deter-
mined, there had to be some disciplined control of the
movement. That was Gandhi's position—after strategy
had been set, it had to be executed under a strongly
structured leadership. We have not had enough of this
degree of discipline in the highly individualistic American peace groups. Muste and I have often argued about
this, and while he often *talks* against an authoritative
chain of command to supervise tactics, he sometimes
acts as if he realizes its necessity quite well. During one
hazardous project, he volunteered for an active role
although, under the circumstances, his participation
would have been most unwise because of his age. He
volunteered, I think, because of his deep concern with
sustaining his status as *the* major leader in actions for
peace. Again, I don't ascribe personal ambition in the
usual sense to him. What motivates him is his recognition that there *has* to be a leader. And realistically, who
but A.J.?"

11

THE CONSCIENTIOUS OBJECTORS

"Whether at Liberty or in Prison, Where These Young Men Are, I Belong."

MUSTE's position as "America's No. 1 Pacifist," as *Time* magazine once called him, was most seriously threatened within the peace movement during the Second World War. While the country was on the edge of war, Muste remained doggedly opposed to violence on either side. Unlike several prominent pacifists, Muste and the F.O.R. did not, however, support the America First movement. "They were essentially isolationist," he explains, "and we were not. We also were convinced that most of those people who didn't want war with Germany would not have objected to war with Japan or Russia. Therefore, theirs was not a clear-cut peace movement, and it would have only confused the issue for pacifists such as myself to have become involved with the America Firsters."

The Fellowship of Reconciliation had been actively educating for peace in churches and schools until America did finally enter the war. It maintained pacifist study groups and sent lecturers to churches, high

schools, colleges, and civic organizations. In the late
1930's, F.O.R. students participated in an annual nationwide Student Strike Against War sponsored by the
Keep America out of War Movement. On October 16,
1940, the first draft registration day, the F.O.R. and
other pacifist groups declared a Day of National Humiliation. Many fasted, and contributed the money
saved to the Fellowship's Food for Europe fund which
was used to protest the British food blockade of Germany and to support pacifists in Europe.

Muste's own troubles in the war were with radical
pacifists in the Civilian Public Service Camps which
had been set up for conscientious objectors whom a
draft board or an appeal officer judged sincere. In the
camps, pacifists were to participate in "work of national
importance" as an alternative to military service. For
the first time, moreover, the government and organized
religious pacifist groups were to be partners in han-
dling conscientious objectors. Committees representing the Friends, Mennonites, Brethren, and other denominations assumed considerable responsibility for
the administration of Civilian Public Service. The major coordinating unit was the National Service Board
for Religious Objectors on which the F.O.R. as well as
the historic peace churches had representatives. Under
the arrangement, the 12,000 men who were to work for
periods of up to six years in the camps received no pay.
Congress had appropriated no funds for payment, and
as it turned out, many of the conscientious objectors—
often with help from their families—contributed to the
cost of their own maintenance.

From the beginning, as Professors Mulford Sibley and
Philip E. Jacob report in their detailed study, *Conscription of Conscience: The American State and the Conscientious Objector, 1940-1947* (Cornell University

Press), many conscientious objectors protested strongly against the system. First of all, a large percentage of Jehovah's Witnesses chose jail rather than the Civilian Public Service Camps. The Witnesses often—though usually without success—sought exemption as ministers, and they regarded alternative public service as a form of yielding to the government the power to curtail their ministerial rights. Furthermore, although over four hundred nonreligious objectors were assigned to the camps, legally a C.O. had to demonstrate religious training and belief to qualify for alternative service. Accordingly, many nonreligious objectors served prison terms. Also among the outcasts were the "absolutists," who opposed any conscripted service, civilian or military. "Consequently," Sibley and Jacob note, "the proportion of the conscientious objectors who populated prisons swelled to approximately three times that in World War I."

In the camps, besides the absence of pay, there was no compensation for an objector's injury or death and no allowance for his dependents. The men were also increasingly bitter because much of the C.P.S. work was hardly of "national importance." In addition, the camps were often in remote areas where there was presumably less danger of the neighboring populace being infected by the pacifist views of the inmates.

Further protests concerned the way in which several of the camps were managed, particularly with regard to increasingly stiff disciplinary measures. The most basic objections to C.P.S., however, have been summarized by Sibley and Jacob as the "military implications in the program and the infringement of freedom resulting from conscription." They add that "the presence of Army officers in the key posts of administration, the awarding of military honors to some of them for their

service in C.P.S. administration . . . and the military
pattern of the regulations prescribed for C.P.S. convinced c.o.'s that the civilian direction assured in the
Selective Service Act had been denied in spirit and practice. . . . Both the c.o.'s and the church were indulging
in fatal collaboration with the 'uncontrolled authority'
of the state."

There were more and more fasts, slowdowns, strikes,
and walkouts which led to jail. Muste and the F.O.R.,
along with other peace group leaders and organizations,
were condemned by the dissidents for having acquiesced
in C.P.S. to begin with and for having continued to support the program. Muste's own thinking shifted during
the war. "I had always," he says, "had great respect for
the absolutist position of refusing to register for the
draft and refusing to accept any alternative service. I
had always backed up those who had taken that position.

"I did believe at the beginning of the war, however,
that the Civilian Public Service Camps, as they had
originally been planned, were a major improvement
over the brutality toward conscientious objectors in the
First War. The work was to have offered a special kind
of pacifist witness and was to have been creative social
work planned in large part by the religious groups administering the camps. It soon became evident that government control of the camps was quite real, not nominal, and that the creative work was in the line of raking
leaves and carrying stones from one place to another.
Moreover, the original concept was for the C.O. to work
freely under no discipline but that of the religious organizations administering the camps. We wound up,
however, simply administering conscription for the government. Selective Service retained full control and laid
down all the rules."

Eventually, Muste admitted he had been wrong. In 1944, after a hard fight and a close vote of its national Council, the F.O.R. was led by Muste to withdraw as an "administrative member" of the National Service Board for Religious Objectors. The F.O.R. remained as a "consultative member" because there was a sizable number of Fellowship members in the camps, and the Fellowship felt a responsibility to look after them.

Muste personally adopted the absolutist position. He advised refusal to register and counseled as well that, if a c.o. did register, he was entirely correct morally in refusing alternative service. He began preaching absolutism in his visits to the camps and indirectly gave support to those conscientious objectors who intended to resist some of the camp rules and to those who planned to walk out.

Even during the period when Muste still had some hope that the C.P.S. system could be made morally tenable, he was constantly trying to negotiate with the government and the cooperating peace groups to improve conditions in the camps. He also tried to mediate between those who ran the camps and the radical conscientious objectors simmering inside. The radicals, however, distrusted Muste because he had originally favored the plan. "There was a great deal of hostility toward him," says Roy Finch, a radical pacifist, and now a Professor of Philosophy at Sarah Lawrence College. "It wasn't until the early 1950's that many of the radical objectors were willing to forget how hostile they had been to Muste during the war."

Dave Dellinger, a nonregistrant in the war, had served in prison and had opposed C.P.S. from the start. He is now—along with Muste and others—an editor of *Liberation,* and his printing plant, Liberation Press, also puts out the magazine. "A.J. did not have an at-

tractive role in those days," says Dellinger. "He was
trying to conciliate groups that were becoming so
basically divergent that he became the target of much
bitterness from both sides. Making it worse were his
own doubts about the system."

"A number of us," recalls one graduate of the C.P.S.
camps, "ended in prison in Lewisburg. In 1942, we were
on a hunger strike that had started as a protest against
racial segregation in the prison and had gone on to
include a demonstration against the prison system in
general, including censorship. An outside mediator was
suggested, but we had become suspicious of most of the
approved mediators. They'd usually come to see us after
having talked to the warden and tell us we were irre-
sponsible. We finally agreed on two moderators we
would accept. One, Evan Thomas, a brother of Norman
Thomas, had suffered terribly in prison during the First
World War, and had opposed any conscription of conscientious objectors in the Second. The other, Julius
Eichel, was editing a magazine called *The Absolutist,* a
title that represented his point of view.

"Muste's name came up. He had written and asked to
come, but we rejected him. Nonetheless, he came. Some
of us didn't even want to see him. It was the damnedest
thing when he did arrive. We stood there and attacked
him, and he kept smiling back at us. Our hostility didn't
seem to reach him. He told us all the factors on the side
of the prison officials, and then he went to the warden
and told him the points he felt we had on our side.
Nothing happened as a result of his intervention. If anything, we felt he'd betrayed us. The hunger strike went
on until a compromise was reached when James Bennett,
Director of the Bureau of Prisons, agreed to make some
changes in the prison rules, principally with regard to
censorship.

Muste has continued to be active in helping conscientious objectors, and has remained consistently absolutist in his own views since the end of the war. He was one of the founders of the Central Committee for Conscientious Objectors in the summer of 1948 and has been co-chairman since February, 1949. Along with the National Service Board for Religious Objectors, the Central Committee helps and advises any conscientious objector who contacts it. The Committee specializes, as its handbook states, "in cases of men who face legal difficulties with Selective Service resulting from deliberate violation of the law as a result of conscience, or those who have difficulty obtaining exemption because they do not fit the narrow, religious Supreme Being requirements of the law."

Although he advises pacifist youngsters of draft age not to register, Muste feels that the current situation for conscientious objectors has improved. "Now, when a registrant is recognized as a c.o. by his draft board, he can usually win assignment to noncombatant military service, or if his principles do not permit that course, to 'civilian work contributing to the national health or safety.' The latter alternative includes choices of service with some government or nonprofit agencies. For example, a c.o. can get a job with the American Friends Service Committee, the Mennonites, and similarly oriented groups to go abroad and do work comparable to that of the Peace Corps. As for nonreligious objectors, few of them get processed any longer. It's a delicate issue, but it appears that for the past several years, the draft boards have just been dodging the problem. They forget the guy. But once in a while they don't, and there are still nonreligious objectors in jail."

Muste, in any case, remains fundamentally opposed to conscription in any form. "Submitting to conscription

even for civilian service," he wrote in 1952, "is permitting oneself to be branded by the State. It makes the
work of the State in preparing for war and in securing
the desired impression of unanimity much easier. It
seems, therefore, that pacifists should refuse to be thus
branded. . . . A decision by the pacifist movement in this
country to break completely with conscription, to give
up the idea that we can 'exert more influence' if we
conform in some measure and do not resist to the utmost
—this might awaken our countrymen to a realization of
the precipice on the edge of which we stand. It might be
the making of our movement."

Five years earlier, Muste had joined a group of radical
pacifists in a ceremony in front of the White House
during which all burned their draft cards. As a preacher,
Muste had none to ignite, but he felt he should be there
as a leading advocate of nonregistration. "The intent of
the demonstration," explained Jim Peck of the War
Resisters League, who did have a card to burn, "was to
get publicity for our position. And since it was a rather
unusual form of protest, we succeeded."

In 1949, when a young Quaker, Larry Gara, was refused bail pending his appeal on a charge of refusing to
register for the draft, Muste wrote *The New York
Times:* "I have been much more active than Larry Gara
and have gone further in trying to promote civil disobedience to the draft act and to any other measures of
preparation for atomic and bacterial war. . . . While not
desiring anyone to take this stand who is not inwardly
prepared to do so, I have done and shall continue to do
all in my power to increase the movement of civil disobedience to the draft among the young and old, men
and women. (In the interest of accuracy, let me make it
clear that I have not promoted civil disobedience as an
officer of the Fellowship of Reconciliation, but as an

individual and also as Secretary of a movement known as Peacemakers. The Fellowship has not engaged in organizing civil disobedience, though its Council and its members give moral support to those who believe they are called to engage in such activities.)

"Furthermore, since January 1, 1948, I have refused to pay Federal income taxes because I felt I had to find every possible means to divorce myself from any voluntary support of the crowning irrationality and atrocity of atomic and bacterial war. . . . I am by no means eager to go to prison; and I bear no ill will to any Federal officials or any one else. But adolescent and growing youth should not be conscripted for atomic and bacterial war. Young men like Larry Gara ought not to be jailed for expressing their deepest religious convictions. . . . Whether at liberty or in prison, where Larry Gara and these young men are, I belong."

Copies of the letter were also sent to the Attorney General and to the Federal District Attorney in New York. Muste had been considering making an antiwar protest through refusing to pay taxes for some time before 1948. He cited the long American heritage of tax refusal, including Thoreau's comment in his essay, *On the Duty of Civil Disobedience:* "If a thousand men were not to pay their tax-bills this year, that would not be a violent and bloody measure, as it would to pay them, and enable the State to commit violence and shed innocent blood. This is, in fact, the definition of a peaceable revolution, if any such is possible."

Muste's decision to act on his beliefs concerning tax refusal was set off by a disagreement within the Fellowship of Reconciliation when Muste's secretary decided she could not conscientiously pay Federal income tax and asked that the F.O.R. not withhold taxes from her pay. After several months of debate within the organization, which led to a referendum of the membership, the majority declared, as John Nevin Sayre has explained, that "the F.O.R. should not break the law except on an issue, such as the refusal to fight in a war, on which all its members agree. We in the majority felt that a person's right not to pay taxes was a matter of individual conscience. We would support that individual, but not to the point of refusing to withhold his or her taxes." Muste was on the losing side.

As an ordained minister, Muste did not have the problem of asking the Fellowship to stop withholding his taxes. Accordingly, in 1948 and each year since, he has simply informed Federal authorities that he is not paying taxes or filling out his return. He was not questioned by Internal Revenue agents until 1951, and he was not brought into court until 1960. He was then charged with owing $1,165 in taxes from 1948-52 as well as additional penalties for "non-filing of returns, for fraud, for non-payment and for substantially underestimating his tax."

John Nevin Sayre and Norman Thomas appeared as character witnesses for Muste, although Thomas disapproved of Muste's position. "I don't think you do any good," says Thomas, "by disrupting organized society. Besides, I doubt if anyone has such complete control over what he does with his money that he can be sure none of it goes to support government activities of which he disapproves. There are, after all, many hidden taxes in what you buy."

Muste's lawyer in his tax refusal campaign has been Harrop A. Freeman, Professor of Law at Cornell Law School. A tax expert, Freeman has also served as attorney for several conscientious objectors. In one of his briefs in the Muste case, Freeman noted: "Taxpayer has no funds. Counsel is not being paid, even for his expenses."

Among Freeman's points for his client were that "It is proper to consider the 'purpose' of a tax in deciding its Constitutionality . . . A person who refuses to make returns or pay taxes solely because of his religious conscience, which he deems protected by the First Amendment, does not incur fraud or other penalties. . . . Petitioner is excused from paying taxes used for war by the First Amendment to the Constitution. . . . Petitioner cannot be compelled to file returns or pay taxes for war purposes under the Internal Revenue Code by virtue of the Nuremberg Principles of International Law." On that last issue, Freeman quotes the Nuremberg Tribunal's reference to the Atlantic Charter in its statement of fundamental principles of law: ". . . the very essence of the Charter is that individuals have international duties which transcend the national obligations of obedience imposed by the individual State."

Muste finally both lost and won his case in the Tax Court. In addition to the tax which the Internal Revenue Service had claimed was due as a result of its examination of F.O.R. payment records, it also pressed its claim that Muste owed further penalties for "fraud" since he had not made out any returns.

As Harrop Freeman explains, "Previous tax refusers had all lost their cases in the District Courts (criminal) and thus there seemed to be a rule that following one's conscience was wrong or criminal. I felt that by going into the Tax Court, which is not handling criminal cases, we would get better treatment and that if we won the fraud issue, this would indirectly help to show that following conscience was not fraud (and perhaps then not criminal). The Tax Court held that A.J. was not guilty of fraud for following his conscience. He did not owe any penalties. It did hold that the tax itself was due. We decided not to appeal this because the fraud decision was in our favor and we might have lost an appeal."

The Internal Revenue Service has threatened Muste with collection of that tax once since the Tax Court decision. There are only a couple of ways, however, in which Muste's funds can be attached. He doesn't have a bank account, nor does he have any property which can be seized. Presumably, the Internal Revenue Service could try to collect the tax out of Social Security or out of a small pension Muste receives. The latter course, some lawyers feel, would be of doubtful validity.

If Muste is ever confronted with the clear choice between paying the tax or going to jail, there is every likelihood that he would choose prison. In a 1954 letter to the Collector of Internal Revenue, Muste wrote: "I do not recognize the right of any earthly government to inquire into my income—or that of other citizens— for the purpose of determining how much they or I 'owe' for the diabolical purpose of atomic and biological war."

As usual, there is disagreement on tactics among pacifists who will not pay taxes. Some will not cooperate with Federal authorities at all. They do not come to court voluntarily, and when they are brought there, they stand mute. Muste respects that kind of absolutism, but does not adopt it himself "because in the main I regard certain institutions of so-called democratic societies as useful and necessary, and because I have wanted to make an effort to secure a judicial determination on the specific issue of whether or not conscientious objection to paying war taxes should be recognized by a democratic government."

Muste also refuses to use the technique of keeping his income down to a point where no taxes are owed. "Keeping one's income down to a subsistence level may be justified," Muste observes, "on the grounds of self-discipline or ascetism, though it is not the pattern of life I have chosen or regard as superior to a less ascetic one. Besides, I do not see how one can in effect recognize that a government may determine one's standard of living or how one can think that permitting government to do so constitutes a significant protest against war taxation."

Muste's uncompromising stand on payment of taxes has encouraged several other pacifists throughout the country to take a similar position. "It's another example," says one of them, "of how A.J. 'leads' the movement, and it also illustrates how he can draw attention to our point of view. When a man as respected as A.J. refuses to pay taxes, it's like Jeremiah walking down the street naked. People stop, look, and listen."

12

IN SEARCH
OF SATYAGRAHA

*"No One Need Wait for Anyone Else in
Order to Adopt a Right Course."*

IN ONE of his earlier letters to the Collector of Internal
Revenue, Muste appeared to be speaking as much to
himself as to the government: "The need for getting our
pacifist teaching off the level of talk and writing and
onto the level of action is, I believe, imperative." This
problem of increasing the number and effectiveness of
action projects against nuclear warfare has increasingly
concerned Muste for the past fifteen years. Accordingly,
he is at the center of many such demonstrations.

In October, 1949, for example, Muste and four other
pacifists staged a sit-down protest in the French Embassy
in Washington. Seven other peace workers picketed on
the sidewalk. All were indignant at the punitive action
the French government was contemplating against
"world citizen" Gary Davis in Paris. The fervent Davis
was being tried and threatened with deportation for
supporting French conscientious objectors in a particularly persistent manner. The French had jailed a leading
native c.o., and Davis had requested he also be jailed.

His offer having been rejected, Davis began a vigil in front of the Cherche-Midi prison, and he was arrested.

The demonstrating American pacifists selected five of their number to take root in the Embassy because, as Muste later told the District of Columbia Police Court, "we felt that on the day when Gary Davis was on trial in Paris, we had to find some symbolic way to be, as it were, on French soil with him and to demonstrate unmistakably our solidarity with him in his trial . . . his effort to gain legal recognition of conscientious objectors in France, and in his renunciation of all war and violence."

French consular officials, amused, politely asked the five to leave. They refused, and when the French started to propel them with gentle but firm hands toward the door, the five "went limp." The technique of "going limp" is a familiar one to some of the more radical pacifists. It involves complete noncooperation with authority. The Washington incident was the first and only time, however, that Muste has used the tactic. "I question," he says, "the effectiveness of the technique in general. In a good many cases, by going limp you divert attention from the particular issue you're trying to dramatize. It is, however, a legitimate element of Gandhian nonviolence, and I respect those pacifists who apply it. Temperamentally though I do not take to being carried places. I did go limp in that one instance because it seemed appropriate at the time. I felt perfectly normal, I must admit, while being carried out to the sidewalk. Since I did it from an inner impulsion, I was quite relaxed. The point of any of these demonstrations is to do what feels most natural to you at the time. It's when you try to be something you're not that you become weak and insecure."

After having been deposited on the sidewalk, one of

the five was arrested for "disorderly conduct" when he told the police he fully intended to return to the Embassy. The other four—along with their seven colleagues —were picked up for illegally demonstrating within five hundred feet of the Embassy. Refusing bond, all twelve stayed in cells overnight. The next morning, all but one pleaded guilty to the picketing charge. Muste as usual was chosen by the group to be its spokesman before the court. He explained the reasons for the demonstration and added: "We had sought in various ways to bring these very important facts to the attention of people. But the ordinary avenues of expression are often shut against news of this kind. Our deepest concern was to make a clear witness against all war. There was an occasion when people told Jesus to rebuke His disciples—"

"Now," the judge interrupted, "you are going way beyond explaining what you are doing."

"This," Muste said with calm stubbornness, "is my last sentence. People wanted Jesus to rebuke His disciples because, they charged, they were 'speaking out of turn.' And Jesus said: 'If these are silent, the very stones will cry out.' There are times like yesterday, your Honor, when men feel under such compulsion of conscience and are unable to keep still. We thank you."

The sentence for each was a $25 fine or thirty days in jail. Having learned that Gary Davis had meanwhile been released in Paris, eleven of the dozen demonstrators, including Muste, paid the fine.

Muste was also traveling widely after the war, attending peace meetings throughout Europe. In lectures, personal contacts, and articles for such international pacifist journals as the British *Peace News,* Muste kept European pacifists informed of American peace workers' attitudes and plans. In December, 1949, Muste made his first visit to India on the occasion of a World Pacifist

Meeting in Sevagram. There he became even more convinced that nonviolent techniques applied on a mass basis could become the most effective way to prevent war. At Sevagram, Muste was enlisted as one of the American members of an international liaison committee to organize a worldwide nonviolence movement.

It was the "sense" of the meeting that *Satyagraha* units be formed in as many countries as possible. "These units," according to a statement of the delegates, "will be composed of those individuals who have full faith in the superiority of nonviolence and moral force over violent methods and who are prepared to discipline their own lives for becoming true *Satyagrahis*. (*Satyagraha* literally means insistence and reliance on Truth or Soul-force.) A *Satyagrahi* is a person who prepares himself for *Satyagraha*. These two words have been chosen because they were coined and made current by Mahatma Gandhi, and there seem to be no other words which could adequately take their place."

The statement continued, quoting Gandhi: " 'In war one inflicts punishment upon the adversary; in *Satyagraha* one draws the maximum suffering on oneself without a trace of bitterness against the opponent as a human being.' " The units were to be active during peacetime in "tackling the roots of violence in social, economic, educational and administrative spheres, such as racial and economic discrimination.

"In organizing nonviolent defense," the statement noted pragmatically, "we will have to stress quality rather than quantity, and unlike military officers, the leaders will be required to be in the front rather than in the rear. There can also be no policy of secrecy in such an organization because nonviolence and truth are integrally related."

Muste had the statement made available to American

pacifists, and added that among the best American ways
to be true *Satyagrahis* were refusal to register under any
conscription law, refusal to pay taxes for war purposes,
and other acts of civil disobedience against preparations
for conflict. Muste tried to rally the skeptical by pointing out that Gandhi had said: "No one need wait for
anyone else in order to adopt a right course. Men generally hesitate to make a beginning if they feel that the
objective cannot be had in entirety. . . . There will
never be an army of perfectly nonviolent people. It will
be formed of those who will honestly endeavor to observe nonviolence."

In a letter to a friend after his return from India,
Muste analyzed Gandhi in terms that can accurately be
applied to himself: "On the one hand, his own motivation was unquestionably religious, always and centrally.
He was constantly striving to purify himself. On the
other hand, he had no hesitation whatever in calling
upon masses of people to practice nonviolence, knowing
perfectly well that they were not doing it from a deeply
religious motivation. He thought for one thing that
political objectives were at times entirely legitimate,
and that it was very much better for people to seek to
achieve them by nonviolence than by violence. Furthermore, he was confident that if people behaved nonviolently, it would develop the nonviolent spirit in
them."

Muste, in any case, continued his own relentless
Satyagraha. In April, 1950, there was a "Fast for Peace"
in Washington. Muste wrote to the F.O.R. staff from the
fast site, Inspiration House: "In case anyone is concerned about my health, I might say that during the
first twenty-four hours of the Fast I had hunger pains
and a fairly amazing headache. I am now nearing the
end of the second twenty-four-hour period. Shortly after

going to bed last night, my headache left me. However, when I awoke this morning I felt an extreme lassitude and after shaving, decided to go back to bed and quickly went to sleep again. The wags around here said I probably had needed such complete relaxation for a long time. . . . Anyway, by 12:30 I felt like getting up and dressing, and except for the fact that I don't feel exactly like running around the block, I feel o.k. I hope there will be no worrying about my health. There are medical experts available here, and if there is any danger, I shall go on a fruit juice diet rather than run serious risks. As . . . evidence of the appeal the Fast has made, we already have word from over 20 cities throughout the country where F.O.R. members and others are engaging in parallel action. And just now a cable has come from . . . Fukuoka, Japan, saying that '64 ministers and youth' are engaging in similar action."

Muste was also stumping the country that year for unilateral disarmament. He had been one of the first leading anti-Communists to adopt that position. "*Threatening* to use nuclear weapons if we mean in some circumstances to use them," he has written, "is in the form of preparation to commit an obscene atrocity. If, on the other hand, we really mean never to use them, then keeping up the *threat* is deceitful. It contributes to confusion and distrust in a tense and troubled world. . . . As the distinguished English Roman Catholic essayist, E. I. Watkin, points out . . . It cannot 'be morally right to threaten immoral conduct.' . . . We are, in fact, told by the Study Commission of the World Council of Churches, and by many other leaders, both Christian and secular, that ultimately we cannot commit the atrocity of mass extermination, in retaliation or in defense of the national existence. Military surrender will be preferable. But if eventually we must abandon faith in nuclear weapons . . . then in God's name why not now? Why not far better now without further delay? What are we—any of us—waiting for?

In a speech to a War Resisters League dinner in 1959, Muste became rather sardonic in answering the proponents of nuclear weapons as a deterrent: ". . . what a brand-new idea it is that weapons—the most intricate, expensive and deadly weapons—are made and stockpiled in an atmosphere of extreme tension, for the purpose of never being used. Each big nation turns out this stuff, we are asked to believe, with no notion of ever using it, but simply in order to keep the other fellow from using his. Surely this is an Alice in Wonderland notion. Raymond Swing long ago characterized this as the theory that 'the bigger the danger grows, the greater the safety.' General Omar Bradley more recently stigmatized it as 'peace by the accumulation of peril.' "

The most formidable objection to Muste's position remains the belief of even many pacifists that not enough Americans can be sufficiently changed in temperament to accept the nonviolent philosophical basis for unilateral disarmament. In 1955, the Quakers issued a pamphlet, *Speak Truth to Power,* which tried to focus on this crucial question. Although a committee of thirteen is listed as responsible for the essay, much of the text is based on a series of memoranda by Muste.

"We disassociate ourselves," the pamphlet states, "from utopianism. Though the choice of nonviolence involves a radical change in men, it does not require perfection." As examples of man's capacity to transcend "the petty, the self-centered, the fearful, and the complacent," *Speak Truth to Power* cites the Indian campaign for independence "in which multitudes of men and women, without being raised to individual sainthood, were able to make an entirely new response to injustice and humiliation . . . ordinary people were enabled to find new courage and self-respect, were able to overcome hostility toward an enemy, and to endure physical suffering, imprisonment and outrages without resorting to violence in return."

Before the majority of people can be reached, the pamphlet continues, there must be "the *unconditional* acceptance of an ideal by a minority," by people such as Thomas Garrett, a nineteenth-century Delaware Quaker. "Haled into court and so heavily fined for his activity in the underground railway that he was left financially ruined, Garrett stood before the Court . . . 'Judge, thou hast not left me a dollar, but I wish to say to thee and to all in this courtroom that if any one knows a fugitive who wants a shelter and a friend, send him to Thomas Garrett and he will befriend him.' Such defiance was regarded then, as it would be regarded today, as a foolish and impractical gesture . . . but . . . it is precisely the demonstration of this kind of unlimited faith that shakes men's souls, and when this happens, the impossible moves nearer to the possible. Garrett's act was politically relevant in the most profound sense because it opened up new dimensions, new power, and new life beyond man's capacity to predict, and the forces thus released served to burst the bonds of practical politics. . . . And so we say to the skeptic of our time: Just as there could be no release from the scourge of slavery, there will be no release from the scourge of war until man's souls are shaken, and this cannot be done save by practicing our faith in men with the same unlimited commitment as did Garrett in his day, and Gandhi in ours."

In conversation, Muste cites growing proof that pacifism can attract a sizable number of converts once a sufficiently committed minority has called dramatic at-

tention to its principles. He lists the rise of pacifist
strength in recent years among American students, professors, and housewives; the remarkable amount of support unilateral disarmament has achieved in Britain; the
establishment for the first time of a pacifist movement
in France as an outgrowth of resistance to the war in
Algeria; and the fact that some church groups in America are giving more support to pacifism than they have
in many years.

"Although, there have been pacifist groups in this
country since the arrival of the Quakers," says Muste,
"it wasn't until the post-1914 years that the major pacifist action groups started. The real wars of previous cen-
turies had taken place elsewhere. We were involved in
the Spanish-American War, but it was a small conflict,
and there was no resultant conscription. Accordingly,
the First World War was a shock."

In an article in *Fellowship,* a journal of the F.O.R.,
Muste has pointed out that not only the F.O.R. but
other pacifist or near-pacifist organizations, such as the
War Resisters League, Women's International League
for Peace and Freedom, the National Council for the
Prevention of War, and the Service Committees of
Friends, Brethren and Mennonites are all post-1914
products. "By 1924, as a result of the widespread revulsion against war that followed World War I and the
almost equally widespread conviction that war could
be prevented and abolished, there was a great upsurge
of pacifism in the churches. In the larger denominations
(with the exception of the Lutheran and, in much less
degree, the Episcopalian), the pacifist position was the
prevalent one among the leaders of theological thought,
in the Student Christian movement, the seminaries and
the upper grades in the Sunday schools."

Pacifist strength in most church groups began to de-

cline markedly, however, with the rise of Hitler. At
the same time, a powerful theological counterpoise to
pacifism resulted from the ascendance of neo-orthodox
thought. The neo-orthodox leaders, Reinhold Niebuhr
among them, included Christian pacifism in their attack
on liberal Christianity and cited it as being prone to
similar errors of perfectionism, utopianism, sentimental-
ism, and political oversimplification.

In the nuclear era, however, there has been a swing
back to pacifism among some church leaders, and Muste
is convinced that return can be accelerated. Among
churchmen as well as lay nonpacifists, Muste still finds
stubborn resistance to the concept of unilateral disarmament. What, he is asked, if the Russian and Chinese do
come and overrun an America that has abandoned nuclear war? Muste's answer is in *Speak Truth to Power:*
"A nation which had disarmed would not in that event
abjectly surrender and let an invader run over and en-
slave it, as is often alleged. On the contrary, it would
have open to it possibilities of nonviolent resistance that
offer more prospects of a creative and genuinely victori-
ous outcome than is the case with violent resistance
under modern conditions.

"Nonviolent resistance, as has been demonstrated on
a large scale in India, and on a smaller scale in many
other places, offers greater promise of confounding and
overcoming an enemy without destroying our values or
our world . . . Any campaign of nonviolent resistance
will include . . . non-cooperation, good will, and nonviolence. The technique is effective because it under-
mines the morale of the enemy and removes his will to
conquer. When a soldier is received kindly, it is hard
for him to continue to hate. When he faces no threat, it
is hard for him to continue to kill. Moreover, he has no
way to compel cooperation when faced with civil dis-

obedience, and without cooperation the enemy will find his existence difficult indeed. All of this is not to suggest that everything would proceed in idyllic fashion and that no suffering would occur in a nonviolent resistance campaign. . . . Obviously, if men are willing to spend billions of treasure and countless lives in war, they cannot dismiss the case for nonviolence by saying that in a nonviolent struggle, people might be killed!"

Muste has long hoped he could accelerate the mass acceptance of nonviolent resistance and unilateral disarmament by political means as well as by protest demonstrations, but he has not been notably successful. He has had no organized political support, however small, since the nonpacifist American Workers Party of the early 1930's. In 1954, Muste tried to gain acceptance in America of the "Third Way International Movement" which had begun in Europe. Its primary purpose, according to its credo, was "to bring together all those who reject the present-day policies of both the Russian and American blocs . . . who refuse to give support to the war preparations of either side in the Cold War, or to any alternative military alliance . . . who are dedicated to waging war on want . . ." Muste was Chairman of the American Third Camp Committee, helped start *Liberation* magazine in 1956 as a forum for Third Camp views, and lectured on the principles of the movement, but the Third Camp eventually dissolved.

Muste has never stopped trying to sway people and governments by such essentially political means as the Third Camp, but particularly during the past decade, his heart has been in nonviolent direct action. A change in his status at the F.O.R. in 1953 enabled Muste to become a much more mobile demonstrator; and the death of his wife in September, 1954, ended his family responsibilities.

13

THE FAMILY

"He Never Did Lay a Hand on Us. Yet He Was a Hell of a Disciplinarian."

As a child, Anna Muste had had rheumatic fever, but there were no indications until 1936 that her heart required special attention. In 1947, her health failed noticeably, and for the final two years of her life, she was an invalid. "The doctors," Muste recalls, "always said she must have been loved very much to have survived as long as she did." During her last years, her husband curtailed his traveling considerably.

Anna Muste was lighthearted and uniquely even-tempered. Helen Norton Starr has observed of the Anna Muste she knew during the Brookwood period that "very few women in the precosmetic age deserved the description 'beautiful.' Anna came very close. While she was alive, she protected A.J. as much as she could from needless distractions and tension. She was his refuge."

Throughout the various stages of her husband's career, Anna Muste was never a public personage. "She was very much herself," Muste says, "and had no particular liking for work within organizational patterns.

She was never really active in the Trotskyite movement when I was, but she did belong to the Fellowship of Reconciliation, which allowed for much more flexibility of viewpoint."

Mrs. Muste was well read, but more in the arts than in politics. A daughter, Connie Hamilton, now married to a farmer and social worker, says that "Mother was not what you would call an intellectual, although she was certainly not the opposite. Her genius was being a wife, mother, and homemaker, and in those roles she far excelled most women. She was the kind of person, moreover, to whom strangers on buses told their troubles. For us as children, she created the atmosphere that contemporary psychologists urge upon mothers. We always knew she was on our side and was interested in whatever we did. We knew that she expected and intended us to do the right thing, and at the same time, we knew for certain that she would always, under any circumstances, love us. I'm sure this was essentially her attitude toward Dad's activities too.

"Moreover, I can't remember a single instance from my childhood that suggested to me that my mother felt the strain of being the wife of a nonconformist who was also away from home a lot. Now that I'm married myself, I have a fairly good idea of some of the strains of the nonconformist life and marriage, and of the terrible, sly temptation to pass them on to your children. I marvel all the more at my mother's self-control. In their own unity, our parents provided an atmosphere of security that has been one of the most significant influences in the lives of all of us."

Nancy Baker, the oldest daughter, the wife of a civil engineer, agrees that her parents enjoyed a remarkably happy marriage. "Mother looked up to Daddy so much. The only thing I couldn't quite understand was the

extent of her patience concerning our family income.
My father never asked for a raise when he was with
the Fellowship, and a couple of times, he even refused
raises. Yet my mother could certainly have used some
help since her health wasn't very good for years. But,
so far as I can remember, she never complained. My
father has always largely ignored money in the sense
that he never seemed worried about what happened
next and didn't care if he didn't have a new suit for
years. We always did live in a decent place and pay our
bills, but there was a time during the Depression when
Mother used to wash the bed sheets because we couldn't
afford to send them to a laundry."

John Muste, currently an Assistant Professor of
English at Ohio State University, can remember his
mother complaining only once. "She was annoyed that
during the Workers Party period Dad had used nearly
all our savings for various things connected with the
cause. She thought he might have held out a little more
for the family."

During his later years at the Fellowship of Reconciliation, Muste not only refused raises but instituted
a system whereby permanent staff members were paid
on the basis of whether they were single or married,
rather than according to their status in the organization.

"I suppose," Connie Hamilton says, "most children
think of their parents as something more than human.
Dad always seemed impregnable to the problems that
ordinary people have. At least, he always seemed able
to surmount them with ease. I still think this is true, but
not in quite so simple a way as I thought when I was
younger. He is certainly much more mature and self-
possessed than most people, not only about world problems, but about his own. This does not mean, however,
that he doesn't feel things deeply. I was hit sharply when

I read his comment in the autobiographical sketches he wrote for *Liberation* that it had never occurred to him that the companion of a lifetime could suddenly be gone. I knew, of course, that he felt it when Mother died, but he showed his feelings so little that his behavior fitted in with my old idea that he could handle such things with the ease and dexterity of a magician. Reading about his shock at losing Mother made me realize that such things could be as hard for him as anybody, even if he does handle his troubles without display."

Anna Muste's friends emphasize her nearly constant cheerfulness. Bayard Rustin describes her as having been "a bundle of giggles. We had some marvelous parties with Anna as hostess. There would be a lot of singing, stories, and some comic monologues from A.J. Anna would goad A.J. to perform, and although she had heard his parody of 'To Be or Not to Be' scores of times, she'd sit back in the corner and giggle again. And of course, many strategy meetings were held in the various homes in which the Mustes lived. Anna would always have something for even the wildest of us to eat and drink, and we felt entirely welcome."

"Insofar as you can gauge parents," adds Rustin, "by how their children turned out, Anna and A.J. were very successful. John, for example, was stricken with and partially incapacitated by polio while in Mexico on his honeymoon, but he finished his work for his master's degree and went on to teach. It's the Muste style. In John, Nancy and Connie, there is the same kind of maturity, dignity and independence that characterized their parents." So independent was John Muste, in fact, that he joined the Navy in the last war.

"My father never put up a fight when I decided to go into the service," says John Muste. "He gave me some F.O.R. stuff to read, and we talked. Since I was only seventeen, he had to sign my papers, and he did without making me feel I'd disappointed him. He didn't withdraw any of his love because I was not taking the same position as he was. I'm still not a pacifist. I can see the logic of pacifism more clearly now than I could then, but I don't consider myself Christian, and to function according to my father's kind of absolute morality, I think you have to be."

"I'm batting .333 with my children with regard to pacifism," Muste says with some regret. "Connie's the only thoroughgoing pacifist. When John decided to go into the Navy, I wasn't too surprised even though he had been a convinced pacifist a few years before. It's true he was going to a Quaker prep school at the same time, but there was really no pacifist influence in the school. I'm afraid that many of the 'better' Quaker schools, the ones that get the children of the well-to-do, are important certainly in the educational field but have lost many of their distinctively Quaker aspects. In any case, nearly all the other kids in John's class were enlisting, and John was not emotionally up to standing apart from what everybody else in his crowd was doing. We felt he should do what he believed."

When Connie Hamilton was once asked how a pacifist father enforced discipline, she answered, "He was the same kind of father before and after he became a pacifist—kind and firm. As a child, I could not even imagine questioning anything he said, although like most children, I could always hope to get around my mother. I was never spanked; I don't think Nancy was either; and I know that John was only once when Mother was goaded beyond endurance. Dad once wrote that we were all angels, and he was perfectly sincere, but quite wrong. We were at least as aggravating as

the average; and with four children of my own, I now
have a very good idea of how aggravating that can be.
Although my father's ideas about political movements
have changed over the years, his ideas about individuals
and what makes *them* move never really have. He respects the individual personality and believes in the
power of love and reason to produce changes in people.
My sister, brother and I were brought up according
to those tenets. My father's pacifism actually had nothing to do with it, because for most of the period when
we were children, he wasn't a pacifist at all."

"He never did lay a hand on us," John Muste con-
firms. "Yet he was a hell of a disciplinarian. I still don't
know how he did it. I guess we were all in awe of him."

"It is true," says A. J. Muste, "that I never struck the
children, but there certainly were situations when I
became tense and lost my temper, to a certain extent.
I've come out of such experiences with the conviction
that in violent conflict between parents and small children, the problem is nearly always with the grown-up.
The child knows when the parent becomes tense and
then is difficult to control. Whenever I've caught myself
in a situation of that sort, I've realized that I was being
aggressive and demanding. When I began to unwind,
the children did."

The Muste family operated within a consistent set
of rules, and when the rules were broken, a discussion
was held. "We never took away their privileges or anything like that," says Muste. "We tried to reason out
the problem. Perhaps the most difficult conflict happened with John. He had decided he wanted to go to
Mount Herman, a prep school in Northfield, Massachusetts. After he arrived, he became terribly lonesome
and wanted to go back to the Friends Seminary he'd
been attending. We felt he ought to see it through
since he had made his choice. I had to go to North-

field to talk with him, and I made it clear he had to stay. It was very tough for him—and for me—but he stuck it out."

Aside from the insistence that their children accept the consequences of their decisions, the Mustes encouraged them to think for themselves. "Our parents," says Connie Hamilton, "never tried to pass on specific opinions to us, but they did teach us to be truthful and to be concerned about other people and what went on in the world. Naturally we picked up some specific points of view, but we were at liberty to accept or reject them or to suit them to ourselves. We were encouraged to ask questions and to discuss anything in which we were interested. Our dinner table was usually the scene of lively discussions, and we children became a pretty articulate trio. Sometimes, I know, we were much too sure of ourselves. One of the things that impressed me about my future husband was that one evening, when he had been invited to dinner, he stood up to all of us in an argument about European political history, and he came out on top."

Alfred Hassler of the Fellowship of Reconciliation has commented that Muste has not only always been a relentless worker for causes, but has also been a good family man—a rather rare combination among full-time idealists. When all the children were still at home, the family once accompanied Muste to a school where he lectured for a couple of months. "We were known there," says Connie Hamilton, "as the family that listened to each other."

Although Muste was often away from the family for considerable periods of time and worked long hours while at home, he frequently read to the children, and taught all three to swim and drive. "He somehow found time," adds John Muste, "to occasionally hit fly balls to me, and we liked to play horseshoes. It was while tossing horseshoes that I learned to swear—from him. Those were about the only occasions when he'd allow himself a few 'damn its.' Whenever he was home, A.J. would also play cards with my mother for an hour or two each evening. He played the game with as much concentration and determination as he gave anything else. One summer his father was staying with us. Grandfather disapproved of card playing and such diversions on Sunday. My parents would wait until he went to bed before indulging in their nightly game of gin rummy."

All the children remember their father's passion for baseball. John accompanied his father to Yankee Stadium several times each season, especially when Bob Feller was pitching. "Years later," John Muste recalls, "when *Liberation* was scheduling a special issue on baseball, my father made a point of asking the other editors not to take the usual intellectual tack and be hard on the game. And the summer he was seventy-four, we sat for hours all the way through a Yankee-White Sox doubleheader that was held up six times because of rain."

At the end of one afternoon of reminiscences about his family, and particularly his parents, John Muste stopped in the middle of a story. "You know," he said, "the basic thing about my father is that whether he's at a ball game or climbing over a fence into a missile base, he's always at peace within himself. He's the *happiest* man I've ever known. I can't believe a man can *be* that happy, but *he* is, he really is."

"A.J. was, however, very lonely for a while after Anna's death," says a close friend. "But there was always his work, and he took on so much of it that I doubt if he allows himself much time now to remember that he is alone."

14

DIRECT ACTION

"We Must Give a Positive and Active Connotation to the Term 'Pacifist.' "

A YEAR before Anna Muste's death, her husband had technically retired at sixty-eight from the Fellowship of Reconciliation. Under the arrangement, which is still in effect, Muste is not obligated to do any work for the Fellowship but can participate in any F.O.R. activity toward which he feels inclined. He is often so inclined, and has, in fact, continued serving as a staff representative for the F.O.R. in the New York City area and is provided by the Fellowship with a secretary. He also represents the Fellowship on a number of committees. Muste's official title now is Secretary Emeritus, and he has a small retirement fund from the Fellowship which will take care of his equally small needs for the rest of his life.

Free from executive responsibility and administrative work, and with all his children married, Muste proceeded to increase his involvement in nonviolent, direct-action projects. Although Muste enjoys nearly all his work, he seems to take most pleasure in the Committee

for Nonviolent Action of which he is national chairman.
In the spring of 1957, Lawrence Scott, a pacifist, formed
an *ad hoc* organization, Nonviolent Action Against
Nuclear Weapons. Scott, like most pacifists of his generation, had been considerably influenced by Muste. He
had first met Muste in Kansas City in 1943 during a
Muste visit that led to the organization there of several
annual institutes on race relations and had resulted in
Scott's own decision to organize a Fellowship House in
the city. Scott had also been impressed by Muste's books,
Non-violence in an Aggressive World (Harper, 1940)
and *Not by Might* (Harper, 1947), which he regarded as
the clearest analyses he had found on the nature and
validity of nonviolence.

The original *ad hoc* committee of about thirty included Jews, Protestants, Catholics; a few nonreligious
actionists; and several Quakers. The committee grew,
and at dawn on August 7, 1957, thirty-five committee
members gathered for a 24-hour prayer and conscience vigil on the twelfth anniversary of Hiroshima in
front of the main gate of the Mercury Project, seventy
miles northwest of Las Vegas. The project marks the
entrance to that part of Nevada set aside for nuclear
testing by the Atomic Energy Commission, and the
vigil was the first demonstration anyone had conducted
at the actual site of a nuclear explosion. After trying
to persuade the guards that atomic testing was unwise
and immoral, eleven pacifists walked into the project,
were arrested, and were given suspended sentences for
trespassing. "The tone of the whole proceeding," *The
New York Times* reported, "was almost amiable."

Muste was not one of the eleven, but in addition to
participating in the 24-hour vigil in the punishing
desert heat, he had prepared the ground for the demonstration by enlisting support from several Las Vegas

ministers and conferring with the state highway police the day before. For the police, Muste had conducted a short course in the theory and practice of nonviolent action.

"You mean," said one officer in evident relief after Muste had finished, "there really isn't going to be a riot?"

Early the next morning, the committee members watched a nuclear explosion from a 25-mile distance. One of them, Albert Bigelow, a former lieutenant commander in the Navy before he became a pacifist, reflected the consensus of his colleagues' opinion after the blast: "This was proof that our intuition, our feeling, and our senses were right. We knew that we could never rest while such forces of evil were loose in God's world." Jim Peck, an atheist, added: "In Las Vegas, among many jumbo-size postcards, I found one depicting a bomb test—with pink-skyed background and all. It was doubtless designed for tourists lured by articles like one that had appeared in *The New York Times* Sunday travel section under the heading: 'Watching the Bombs Go Off.' I didn't feel like sending one."

The next major project of the action group, which had become the Committee for Nonviolent Action, was the voyage of the *Golden Rule,* an attempt to sail a thirty-foot ketch into the Eniwetok nuclear bomb testing area in the Marshall Islands where a series of tests had been scheduled for April, 1958. There had been forerunners—in theory—of the peace ship. During the Second World War, several young pacifists prepared a boat for a trip to Japan as a dramatic gesture to help bring peace. Pacifists in Japan had been contacted by their American counterparts through a roundabout route suggested by Quaker peace workers. Muste was one of the advisers for the project, but it never materialized. When the atomic bomb was dropped on Hiroshima, the idea was abandoned since the war was clearly over.

In the spring of 1957, a British Quaker, Harold Steele, tried to organize a protest expedition to Christmas Island, 1,000 miles south of Hawaii, where the British were planning nuclear tests. Steele was stymied in Tokyo, but his example fired a number of American pacifists to go ahead with a similar plan of their own. Lengthy preparations, in which Muste was intimately concerned as strategist and fund raiser, were made for the voyage of the *Golden Rule,* and four members of the Committee for Nonviolent Action finally set sail from San Pedro, California, on the first 2,500 miles of a projected 4,500-mile journey. They arrived in Honolulu on April 19, 1958. Five days later, the United States Attorney successfully asked the Federal Court in Hawaii for an order restraining the *Golden Rule* and its crew. On May 1 the temporary restraining order was turned into a preliminary injunction. Nonetheless the *Golden Rule* sailed on that day about an hour after its crew had left court. Some two miles offshore, the pacifist sailors were placed under arrest by the Coast Guard. The crew refused bail as a matter of principle, and the men spent six days in jail waiting trial. A subsequent sentence of sixty days was suspended, and a year's probation was added.

On the mainland, Muste and others helped organize protest demonstrations. Throughout the country, picket lines encircled Federal buildings and branch offices of the Atomic Energy Commission. As Albert Bigelow, captain of the ship, says in his book, *The Voyage of the Golden Rule* (Doubleday, 1959): "Most of these people had never been in a public demonstration or picket line before. Few would have described themselves as 'pacifists.' Many, in person and by petition . . . tried to share more fully in our action. . . . They showed that the A.E.C. order also branded as criminals any U.S. citizens who 'conspired with' or 'acted in concert' with those who would enter the bomb-test area. These men and women submitted evidence of active support of the *Golden Rule,* such as receipts for cash contributions. In San Francisco alone, 432 persons petitioned the U.S. Attorney to take action against them. They said that if the crew of the *Golden Rule* were guilty, so were they."

A "Walk for Peace Committee" was formed (A. J. Muste, chairman) with the cooperation of the American Friends Service Committee, *The Catholic Worker,* the Fellowship of Reconciliation, Peacemakers, the War Resisters League, and the Women's International League for Peace and Freedom. The walkers rallied in front of the White House on Memorial Day weekend. There were also attempts by the C.N.V.A. to get several of its members visas for Russia where they planned parallel demonstrations against Soviet nuclear tests. "We are no longer content," the committee announced, "to work only in conventional ways by which we have been unable to persuade our fellow citizens and political leaders. We mean now to speak with the weight of our whole lives." The visas never came.

In Honolulu, meanwhile, the crew decided to appeal their sentence and delay their next sailing until the case was heard. The crew was divided as to whether waiting was the wisest course, and there was pressure from the Committee for Nonviolent Action in New York. Muste particularly felt that the *Golden Rule* was an action project and that time should not be wasted in legal processes. He came to Honolulu to coordinate C.N.V.A.'s views with those of the crew and also to rally support in the community and assist in the court proceedings.

The *Golden Rule* was set to sail again on June 4. Ten minutes before departure time, Bigelow was arrested for "criminal conspiracy." The ship sailed without him. Nearly six miles out, two Coast Guard cutters forced the *Golden Rule* to stop and arrested its crew, although technically the ship was outside the three-mile limit of American jurisdiction. The Coast Guard acted under the doctrine of "hot pursuit," which maintains that a criminal can be pursued across a border and legally captured.

There were no further sailings of the *Golden Rule*, but another ship, the *Phoenix*, followed its example. The new interloper was manned by Earle Reynolds, an anthropologist, his wife, and their two children. The *Phoenix* did penetrate the testing area before the 1958 tests had ended, but was forced to leave by the Navy and the Coast Guard.

A. J. Muste and most other pacifists believe the voyage of the *Golden Rule* and the epilogue by the *Phoenix* were the most successful of all direct-action demonstrations to that point because the dramatic nature of the sailings brought the movement unprecedented international publicity.

"Golden Rule said," Albert Bigelow emphasizes, " 'We are not telling you *what* to think, but we are saying in the most dramatic way we can that there is a *need* to think.' " Over a thousand letters from many countries were received by the crew while they were in prison in Hawaii. One from a Hawaiian legislator said: "The *Golden Rule* shall always remain with me as one of the highest points in my life. I never knew how deeply I could feel for my fellow men. . . . Knowing

that there must be others who will fight gives me faith in the future."

Muste is familiar with the view that demonstrations such as the *Golden Rule* are unrealistic. "Actually," Muste disagrees, "the *Golden Rule* was an important element in the peace education of great numbers of people. It also gave a positive and active connotation to the term 'pacifist.' The cumulative effect of all these projects and vigils is to bring into work for peace thousands of people who would never before have thought of engaging in any sort of demonstration. A movement becomes very different in character and in its effect on the noncommitted when it can get people out onto the street confronting authority. Also, demonstrations bring us much more publicity than any other technique. I do not say that nonviolent action is the only form of useful action for peace, but it's an extremely important part of the educative process that is our essential aim."

Muste is also aware of the criticism of direct-action projects from some religious pacifists who regard these demonstrations as undignified. "As a person who has one foot in the church and the other one somewhere else," Muste observes, "I find myself chiding church people for not getting out on the street. When they tell me that there are too many beards among the demonstrators and that the impression is of a beatnik picnic, I tell them that if they want the image changed, they can join the line. It's difficult to find converts, however, in the church. The church has become so middle class and respectable that most of its members have a huge block against being part of direct-action projects."

Another project of the Committee for Nonviolent Action in which Muste became thoroughly involved was Omaha Action in the summer of 1959. Bradford

Lyttle, an absolutist pacifist, was one of the leaders of the demonstration and recalls that "as usual, A.J. was enormously helpful in dealing with the ministers, the press, and other elements of the community. For one thing, he so obviously looks like your father, and his attitude is so understanding and unaggressive that he can make contact with almost anyone. We started preparations early in 1959. Our target was the missile base in Mead, Nebraska, thirty miles southwest of Omaha. The first C.N.V.A. demonstration at a missile base— one in which A.J. did not take part—had taken place in Cheyenne, Wyoming, the summer before."

Before the civil disobedience at Mead, there were public meetings in Omaha, distribution of pamphlets, and peace walks to Mead from Omaha and Lincoln, Nebraska. The band of actionists maintained a vigil outside the Mead base for a month. On July 1, the morning of their nonviolent invasion, Muste, the first scheduled to climb over the fence into the restricted area, spoke to the crowd of the curious, the hostile, the converted, the police, and the press. He made clear his feeling that the action he was about to take was, in his own case, religiously motivated. Softly but firmly, Muste quoted at length from Isaiah: "For thus said the Lord Jehovah, the Holy One of Israel. In returning and rest shall ye be saved; in quietness and confidence shall be your strength. And ye would not: but ye said, No, for we will flee upon horses; therefore shall ye flee: and, We will ride upon the swift; therefore shall they that pursue ye be swift."

When Muste began to speak, there was some jeering from the crowd, but he soon commanded complete attention. Finally, he stepped up to the $4\frac{1}{2}$-foot fence, and slowly climbed over. Muste and the other fourteen who broke the law had to climb the barrier twice. According to regulations, anyone trespassing on a mili-

tary reservation must first be asked by the commander
of the base or his representative to leave. If the tres-
passer refuses, he is then arrested. Muste climbed down
on the proscribed side of the fence, was presented with
a letter from the commander, and was ushered out
through the gate. Muste read the letter, stepped to the
fence, climbed over once more, and was placed under
arrest.

Muste rejected bail, and spent nine days in an Omaha
jail. "He had a hard time," notes the much younger
Brad Lyttle. "It was hot, and the jail was a real hole.
The food was terrible; A.J. was allowed no exercise; and
only relatives were allowed to visit, but he had none
there. By the end of his time, he was exhausted. I've
never seen him so tired. Yet he remained unemotional.
He betrayed how worn out he was only by the fact
that his hands, which shake anyway, were shaking much
more than usual. His pallor was marked, but his spirit
was whole even though the guards had treated him with
curt disrespect."

Muste was given a suspended sentence and placed
on probation on condition that he promise not to
climb the fence again. Since he felt he had made his
witness, and besides had commitments in Africa, he
took the suspended sentence. The pre-trial stay in jail
was not a unique experience for Muste. As a labor
leader and later a radical pacifist, he had been imprisoned a number of times. A schoolmate of John
Muste remembers the boy saying occasionally during
the early 1930's: "Well, it's probably time for Dad to
be in jail again."

Muste's calm remains unbroken in jail. He reads,
or jokes with his cellmates, and waits for bail, if he has
decided to accept bail. During one incarceration in
1955, as an aftermath of the first civil defense protest
action in New York, Muste and several pacifists, includ-

ing a young, eager F.O.R. apprentice, were held over-
night. In the morning, the youngster rushed to where
Muste was sitting, absorbed in the sports pages of *The
Times*.

"Let's get up a statement, A.J.," he said impatiently.
"We really ought to be working on one right now."

Muste looked up. "Relax. We'll get one ready later."
And Muste returned to the box scores.

The demonstrators were bailed out, and that afternoon, at his office, Muste did compose a press release.
"A.J. works hard," an associate of his in the War Resisters League noted at the time, "but he works at his
own speed. In many areas, not all of them ideological,
he is a man who will not be pressured."

Muste's children and several of his friends wish he
could be induced to lessen the kind of activity that
does occasionally place him behind bars. Connie Hamilton is torn between her radical pacifist convictions and
her worries about her father's well-being. "I do feel,"
she says, "that Dad and people like him are the criers
in the wilderness who may or may not be heard but
who are among the few people talking real sense in
this age. But when he gets involved in demonstrations
in the desert, for example, I am also terribly concerned
about whether he will get edible food and reasonably
good treatment in jail. He is a remarkable man for his
age, of course, and his good health all his life is probably
as much a tribute to his sound mental health as to his
original physical equipment. But even though he ages
slowly, he *is* seventy-eight, and I get more and more
worried about him. When I was a child, I was convinced
that he was literally indestructible. Later, I felt that he
was emotionally and intellectually indestructible. Now
I know that he is far, far sounder than most people,
but nobody is that indestructible."

Dave Dellinger, an associate of Muste on *Liberation,*
believes that "part of A.J.'s acceleration of activity in
recent years results not only from his greater mobility
upon retiring from the F.O.R. but also from his recognition that he hasn't too many more years to live. I've
never known him to be so daring as in the past few
years. He has become much more than the organizer
and reconciler. And now that he is doing more direct-
action work, he seems more relaxed and more informal.
His sense of humor was always evident, but it's become more pungent. He's also aware that his own following has grown, and that he's reaping the harvest of
a long life. He's always had personal supporters, but
as the times changed and he changed with them, the
number of Musteites in the peace movement has in-
creased."

Muste rejects the theory that he has changed appre-
ciably since becoming Secretary Emeritus of the F.O.R.
"I'm still a reconciler. One has to be both a resister and
a reconciler to be an effective pacifist. You have to be
sure that when you're reconciling, you're also resisting
any tendency to gloss things over; and when you're
primarily resisting, you have to be careful not to hate,
not to win victories over human beings. You want to
change people, but you don't want to defeat them. I
doubt that I've become more radical in the past ten
years. Certainly, however, as the time grows short for
all of us, our work for peace has become more intense.
This is a period of nuclear pacifism. I do not think
though that my own feeling of urgency is at all due to
intimations of my demise. I seem to be quite relaxed
on that score. I don't think I'd work any harder if I
knew exactly when I were going to die. I guess, in fact, I
couldn't work much harder than I do now."

15

DEALING
WITH THE
COMMUNISTS

*"We Are to Love Them, but I Do Not
Take This to Mean That We Have to Work
with Them Politically or Be Sentimental
and Naïve About Certain Aspects of Their
Behavior and Strategy."*

ALONG WITH his activities for peace, Muste remains absorbed by the possibilities of broadening and energizing the American Left. He no longer feels, however, that a third party is currently a viable goal. "The establishment in the United States of a new party," Muste said in 1962, "is hedged with so many obstacles that the attempt to do it seems a waste of energy."

He does believe, on the other hand, that those who are profoundly dissatisfied with both parties can find a place for their energies and skills in the nonviolent movements for peace and social dislocation. In the process, they may ultimately be able thereby to alter existing power structures. For this to happen, however, the lines of communication must be kept open between the radical peace movement and all other groups who are "breaking loose from 'business as usual.'"

Particularly revealing of Muste's logical, unsentimental, and non-naïve approach to the challenge of keeping the lines open has been his attitude toward American Communists, past and present. During the 1950's, Muste was one of the very few anti-Communist radicals to suggest that it might be possible (particularly after Khrushchev's repression of the Hungarian revolt) to get some American Communists to reconsider their views. Starting around 1955, he initiated a series of private conversations with a few Communists, among them several who later left the party. The latter, although they do not ascribe their break with Communism to Muste's influence, do feel, as John Gates, former editor of the *Daily Worker* says, that the conversations did make them feel that someone on the outside understood their problems.

"It was a considerable help," says Gates, "to be able to talk frankly with someone who wasn't trying to proselytize us. We had been trained to believe that there couldn't be anything decent or honest in 'liberals' who weren't in the party, but it was revealing to recognize the thread of principle that ran through everything a man such as Muste said and did. Most of the other non-Communists were thoroughly suspicious of those of us who were having doubts about the party. James Wechsler of the *New York Post* said to me after I'd left the Communists that he never thought someone like me could really make the break. 'Never in a million years,' he said. But Muste did think our reexamination of our political beliefs was genuine. He had confidence in us. I still think his own radical views are too isolated from what the great masses of people are feeling so that he'll continue to be frustrated as a politician. I'm convinced

we're going to accomplish more through the Democratic
Party than through any splinter groups. But I don't
underestimate what Muste has done in making church
groups more aware of civil rights and the peace movement. That part of his contribution is huge. And his
personal example has been enormously impressive. I
say this as an atheist, but if I were to be asked if I've
ever known a saint, I'd have to say Muste comes close."

Muste's willingness to try to establish communication
with Communists has occasionally led to sharp criticism
of him from within the peace movement and from outside. There was resistance to his public debates with
Communists, starting at the end of 1955, and to his
initiating a petition to President Eisenhower asking
amnesty for Communists who had been jailed under
the Smith Act. The petition, for which Muste obtained
support from Norman Thomas, Eleanor Roosevelt, and
others, asked suspension of further prosecutions under
the law until the Supreme Court had reconsidered it.

Muste opposed any "united front" activity with Communists or Communist sympathizers, but did insist that
Communist views should be heard and their civil rights
protected. "As Christians—or on other grounds—in our
personal and other relations," Muste wrote in 1956,
"Communists are to us human beings, members of
the one human family, children of God. We are to love
them, but I do not take this to mean that we have to
work with them politically or be sentimental and naïve
about certain aspects of their behavior and strategy.
To love a fellow man does not require that we cooperate
with him in lying or exploiting others or some other
evil thing. It requires the opposite, that we do not
cooperate in these things, that we do not let him live,
if he is so living, under the delusion that these things
are good. It means that we love him even while he does

evil, believe that he is capable of redemption, try to call on 'that of God' in him. To love, to be truly human, is always to deal with others on the basis of reality."

The Federal Bureau of Investigation, however, did not take a kindly view of Muste's association with Communists. In February, 1957, Muste and nine other non-Communists had attended the Communist Party convention as impartial observers and unprecedentedly had been permitted to sit on the floor with the official delegates. Opposing factions in the party, led by William Z. Foster and John Gates, were in a struggle for power, and Muste thought it important to observe empirically what changes, if any, would result from the debate at the convention. Muste and some of the others present, Dorothy Day of the *Catholic Worker* and Lyle Tatum of the American Friends Service Committee among them, felt that the proceedings had been "democratically conducted" but suspended judgment as to whether the party actually had started in the direction of being independent of Moscow.

In March, 1957, J. Edgar Hoover placed in the record of the Senate Internal Security Subcommittee the charge that the "impartial observers" had been handpicked and "were reportedly headed by A. J. Muste who has long fronted for Communists and who recently circulated an amnesty petition calling for the release of Communist leaders convicted under the Smith Act."

Muste wrote a long letter to Hoover, denying that he had ever "fronted" for Communists. "Not only," Muste made it clear, "was I not connected with any Communist fronts . . . but I took a leading part as the executive secretary of the F.O.R. in analyzing and exposing the dangerous and fraudulent character of 'united fronts' and in persuading the F.O.R. groups both here and in other countries not to take part in such activities as the World Council of Peace and its affiliated groups, the Stockholm Peace Petition, etc. What criticism there has been in pacifist and other peace groups during those years was to the effect that I was too 'rigid' and perhaps 'unreconciling' about such matters. To what pass have we come if a single individual—and he the head of the FBI presumably charged in a special and delicate manner with the protection of citizens against attack and the defense of our liberties—can make charges against an individual in the casual manner that you have used in this case?

"I raise this question not, except in a very minor degree, on my own behalf. I do have some means of publicity and a long public record of being open and above board in what I do, whatever views people may hold as to my behavior. . . . We are taught in the Scripture . . . that it is the business of those who have influence or power to be specially considerate of the weak and to 'take care not to offend one of these little ones.' There are, alas, a good many people in this country who have little if any means to defend themselves, who have been injured, materially and spiritually, by those who have power and prestige. . . . I hope that I may hear from you. If you should have time to discuss these matters with me on a personal basis, I should appreciate it. I should perhaps make it clear that I am conscientiously opposed to responding to summons to appear before any government official or agency engaged in investigating the political or religious opinions of myself or others."

There was no answer from Mr. Hoover.

Sidney Lens, also a longtime anti-Communist, was among the observers at the convention. "The irony of Hoover's attack on A.J.," Lens says, "is that A.J. has been one of the most effective opponents of Communism in this country. It's largely because of him that the Communist Party was not able to take over the peace movement here in the past decade. Protégés of Muste, moreover, were vital in organizing the National Committee for a Sane Nuclear Policy, which helped cut the ground from under the phony peace strategy of the Communists. He isn't active in it, because it hasn't come out for unilateral disarmament. Others influenced by Muste, such as Martin Luther King and former colleagues of Muste in the F.O.R., have made it equally difficult for the Communists to move into the campaign for racial integration."

"It's true," says John Gates, "that if it hadn't been for Muste, there might well have been a vacuum in the peace movement into which we could have moved." Reverend Claud D. Nelson of the National Council of the Churches of Christ adds, concerning Muste, that "We have had no surer guide as to Communist strategy and no more effective counsel in preventing entanglement, actual or apparent, in Communist strategy conducted under the mask of the search for peace."

Actually, Muste's own involvement years before in radical politics had made him a uniquely qualified pacifist organizer. "He certainly became," says one Communist rather ruefully, "a *practical* idealist."

After his skirmish with J. Edgar Hoover, Muste went on to create a furor in pacifist and radical circles by launching in May, 1957, the American Forum for Socialist Education, a series of conferences and debates in various cities in which Communists and non-Communists participated. Roger Baldwin opposed the project, terming it "another aspect of A.J.'s romanticist nonsense." Baldwin hasn't changed his mind. "Well," he said several years later, "A.J. was once an active minister of the Gospel so that you can expect almost anything from him. He keeps hoping for the best, and certainly a dialogue is no crime, but I didn't see any sense to it."

"It's not only," said a supporter of the American Forum, "that you can't ever take the preacher out of A.J., but you can't remove the Marxist radical from the preacher."

Norman Thomas, who had been severely stung in the past by inroads of factionalist radicals into his party, also opposed the American Forum. "It was a premature move on A.J.'s part. The Forum gave some of those Communists the false impression that they could remain in the party and still be accepted in the community. The Communists don't belong in jail, but they also don't belong in any party with which I want to be connected."

Robert Gilmore, former New York secretary of the American Friends Service Committee, feels, however, that the American Forum "did establish the Communists as human beings. If only in that respect, A.J. made a major contribution to the thinking of some of us."

Many left-wingers, including key figures in the Socialist Party and *Dissent* magazine, objected to the American Forum because Muste included Communists on its committee alongside such anti-Communists as Dorothy Day of the *Catholic Worker* and Sidney Lens. Several newspapers were exercised, and the *New York Post* called the Forum a new "united front" of "Communists and some leftists." In *Liberation,* Dave Dellinger, who supported the Forum, told the story of "the anti-Communist who was arrested at a May Day demonstration while carrying a picket sign denouncing Stalin. As he was being put into the paddy wagon, he protested that he was an anti-Communist. 'I don't care what kind of a Communist you are,' said the arresting officer. 'You get in that wagon.' "

Muste was genuinely perplexed at the fierce opposition to his American Forum. "People like Norman Thomas thought the Forum, by giving Communists a platform, would afford the party a chance to revive itself and confuse people politically. It's an odd point of view to believe that such discussions would lead to the strengthening of the Communists. One wonders whether those who object on that ground don't feel somewhat inferior in their capacity to uphold their own positions. In any case, in our two years of American Forum meetings, we did establish some communication between differing viewpoints and we did make contact with people in the Communist Party itself—John Gates, Doxey Wilkerson, Albert Blumberg—who were rethinking their position, and later did leave the party."

Soon after the American Forum was launched, the Internal Security Subcommittee of the Senate announced that it was investigating the Forum. Under the instructions of Senator James Eastland, subpoenas were issued to five persons connected with the Forum, and a letter was sent to Muste, the Forum's chairman. Muste wrote Eastland that he would refuse on principle to answer any of his questions and added that while he also believed no government agency had the right to investigate Eastland's own political activities either, the Senator's stands on integration in the public schools and on other aspects of race relations "constitute an immense threat to the security and good name of the United States and certainly give a major assist to Communist propaganda."

Muste was not called before the Subcommittee. J. Edgar Hoover's distortion of Muste's record does, how-

ever, continue to be cited in attempts to discredit the
nonviolent movement for integration and peace. In
1961, after Jim Peck had been savagely beaten in Ala-
bama during a Freedom Ride, that state's attorney
general, MacDonald Gallion declared on an NBC television show that Peck was a "Communist associate."
The charge was wholly untrue, but it is indicative of
the long-term fallout from erroneous Hoover attacks
that among the "evidence" provided by Gallion was the
fact that Peck was an active member of the Committee
for Nonviolent Action. "The group is headed," Gallion
continued, "by A. J. Muste who has a long record of
association and cooperation with identified front
groups."

The next year, an attempt was made to discredit the
peace movement as a whole by syndicated columnist
Jack Lotto through the exaggerated charge that "most
of its demonstrations are led by the Committee for Nonviolent Action." Lotto, whose work appears in the
Hearst press, went on to identify Muste, "Coordinator
of the C.N.V.A.," as the "guiding force" behind many
of these protests. Naturally at that point J. Edgar Hoover's description of Muste followed. The final implica-
tion was that all direct action for peace becomes—
however unwittingly—part of a grand Soviet design.

In 1960, Muste became involved in another controversy concerning Communists. This dissension did
not involve the question of whether a dialogue with
them was possible but rather with the proper course for
the peace movement when it is threatened from without
by the accusation that it has become infiltrated by Communists.

By the spring of that year, SANE (Committee for a
Sane Nuclear Policy) had grown in numbers and, to
some degree, in prestige since its founding in 1957. A

SANE rally had been scheduled for Madison Square Garden on May 19 at which Alfred Landon, Walter Reuther and the late Eleanor Roosevelt were to speak. Two weeks before, Senator Thomas Dodd, vice-chairman of the Senate Subcommittee on Internal Security, threatened to attack SANE on the basis that Communists occupied some influential posts in the organization.

The resulting crisis is worth exploring because it caused a deep split within the peace movement and further underlined the consistency of Muste's own views concerning the basic principles such a movement must maintain. Henry Abrams, who had been in charge of promotion for the rally and who in the past had been active in the American Labor Party and in the 1948 Wallace presidential campaign, was the first member of SANE summoned by the Subcommittee. Abrams refused to answer questions and took the Fifth Amendment.

Soon after, Norman Cousins, co-chairman of SANE, asked Abrams if he would tell Cousins himself whether or not he was a Communist. Abrams refused on principle, but did say he would give Cousins or anyone else his assurance that he made his own decisions and took guidance from no organization or individual. (In a *Liberation* series on the issue, Muste made clear that he had investigated and discovered it was possible Abrams might have once been a Communist. "On the other hand," Muste continued, "he was more recently engaged in some political activity which the C.P. opposed. I am mentioning these matters, partly to indicate to members of SANE that I am aware of 'problems' in this situation, but even more in order to make it perfectly clear that in any case I adhere to the positions taken in this article.")

Cousins removed Abrams from office in SANE. He also asked Senator Dodd, a friend, to hold off his attack until after the Madison Square Garden rally. There is considerable confusion as to the nature of anything else discussed between SANE executives and the Subcommittee. Six days after the rally, however, Dodd declared in a Senate speech that Cousins had "asked for the Subcommittee's assistance in ridding SANE of whatever Communist infiltration did exist. He offered to open the books of the organization to the Subcommittee and to cooperate with it in every way." (Cousins later denied that any names had been turned over to or received from Dodd and that any commitments had been made by either side.)

Dodd, in any case, did attack SANE after the rally, and was answered publicly by that organization: "As a matter of democratic principle and practice we resent the intrusion of a Congressional Committee into the affairs of an organization which during its entire life has acted only in according with its declared principles. . . . The Committee [SANE] itself is entirely capable of carrying out its principles and guaranteeing that it will not permit their betrayal or subversion under any pressure from, on the one hand, investigations directed to its hurt, or on the other hand, by the actions of its local chapters or their leaders."

The fact remained, however, that one man had already been driven out of SANE under circumstances which many civil libertarians would have questioned and that a diligent move was underway by SANE officials to expel any individuals or chapters who seemed to be controlled either by Communists or their sympathizers. Suspects would be questioned and removed if their answers were unsatisfactory. Several notables in SANE—Linus Pauling and Robert Gilmore, among them—resigned. Some of the New York City SANE groups, moreover, decided to form their own Greater New York Conference of Peace Groups which would function independently of SANE. The Dodd incident and its follow-up by SANE also lost the organization the support of many students and other young people as well as most of the radical pacifists.

Muste became the spokesman for many of the dissidents when he sharply criticized SANE for what he termed its "grave error" in handling the situation. Referring to Senator Dodd's threat to imperil the success of the Madison Square Garden rally, Muste wrote: "Surely, in view of experience with individuals and Congressional committees engaged in political inquisition, and on the basis of elementary democratic principle, the only way to have dealt with the Senator would have been to tell him to drop his bomb, if he regarded that to be his duty and a virtuous act. It would have been, furthermore, to attack the principle on which such committees operate and to join with those who have called for their abolition by Congress, assuring Senator Dodd that this would have been one of the emphases to be introduced into the program of the rally. Dodd should also have been told that SANE would defend Abrams against the Subversive Activities Committee and assert his Constitutional right to plead the Fifth Amendment before such a Committee, whatever personal views SANE leaders might hold about the *wisdom* of such a plea.

"Instead," Muste continued, "Norman Cousins, a good, brave and educated man instantly feared what an attack by Senator Dodd might do to SANE. If this is the effect on such a man, imagine what fear does to ordinary people in a society where conformism is a dominant element. Moreover, fear in the presence of this phenomenon is just the way not to react to it. It feeds on fear and becomes more menacing. This fear inhibits the confrontation of unorthodox ideas, whether 'subversive' or not, by individuals, and by voluntary associations, which is the only way in which erroneous or dangerous ideas can be effectively dealt with."

Muste pointed out that the issue was not that of co-operating with Communists in the peace movement. "It is clear that in this country there can be no effective peace movement which is under the control of the C.P. or which is in any sense an instrument of the Soviet Foreign Office." There can be, he also emphasized, no unity with those who "do not accept our view that individuals should break with war and that one government cannot excuse its testing and its nuclear war build-up on the ground that another government refuses to agree to stop these criminal actions." It is, furthermore, "romantic, unrealistic and un-Marxian to assume that an arsenal of H-bombs is only so much hardware, the existence of which does not affect the very nature and structure of any state or other organization which manufactures and maintains such power to commit military aggression." So much for the line that the Soviet Union heads the "peace-loving" power bloc.

Therefore, Muste went on, "If a person in a SANE group were known to be a card-carrying member of the C.P. or over a period automatically followed its line, it would be entirely proper for the officers of a group to talk with such a person and point out that he does not properly belong in SANE. If such a person did not withdraw, I think the matter should be frankly discussed in the group with this person present." But, Muste added, we are talking "about specific cases of known present C.P. members, or consistent followers of the C.P. line, not persons accused of being Communists or pro-Communists by Congressional committees.

"The basic decision," Muste continued, "which has to be made by organizations working for peace in seeking to maintain their own integrity and consequent effectiveness—as all private organizations certainly have a right to do—is between defining their programs, pronouncements and activities so clearly as against testing or other nuclear preparation by *any* nation that those who really cannot accept that stand find the organization uncongenial and not useful for their purposes; *or else* to institute some system of loyalty oath and screening. It seems to me that the former is the sound course. . . . If, in order to guard against a state of constant suspicion because there may be people in the group who have ulterior motives, procedures are instituted which tend to put everyone under suspicion, the poison that drains the life of the organization has not been reduced but rather aggravated."

Muste then returned to his preoccupation with keeping lines of communication open. "We are living in a new period, and many people are in the process of revising their thinking and their associations. A good many former Communists and sympathizers are essentially sound people: it should not be necessary at this hour to argue against the idea that they will be Stalinists at heart forever. In Poland, Hungary, and elsewhere, it has been demonstrated that some of them never were. Moreover, many of these people are highly capable and trained for organizational work. It would seem a serious loss if they were barred from using these skills in the cause of peace. But if they find in a peace organization the same kind of dogmatism, suspicion, and obsession with orthodoxy that finally drove them out of the C.P., or its fronts, they will stop working. It would seem, therefore, that an organization which has clearly defined its purpose in the manner I have already suggested, could judge such people on the basis of actual performance rather than by subjecting them to a loyalty test in advance."

The dispute finally subsided, but Muste has remained skeptical of the root effect of such groups as SANE which are essentially organizations of liberals. "We share the position," he states, "that an effective United States peace movement cannot be built by people who are emotionally pro-Soviet or pro-Communist and who do not apply the same standard of judgment to Soviet power politics and nuclear military measures that they apply to the policies and military preparations of the American power state. . . . But the other side of this is that a sound and effective peace movement at the present juncture in world affairs has to apply the same standards of judgment to U.S. cold warriors, U.S. nuclear policy and nuclear-war preparation as to their Soviet counterparts. And one very important reason why organizations such as SANE experience great difficulty in dealing with the 'Communist' and 'fellow-traveler' problem is that their own ideological position is unclear or faulty.

"In large measure," Muste went on, "the liberals on whom SANE seeks to build still think in nationalistic terms and cling to the 'deterrence' concept with all that this implies. They have not arrived at the stage of radical criticism of the U.S. politico-economic regime and realization of the profound changes that will have to take place in it, if nuclear war is in fact to be averted. It is in this kind of context that they work for cessation of testing and 'serious' disarmament negotiation. . . . They do not fully and clearly accept the thesis that 'war is the enemy' and must be resisted in all its forms and in every land.''

For all of his attempts to keep communication alive between diverse groups, Muste has consistent trouble in relating to liberals, not only in SANE but in religious movements as well. An echo of the SANE controversy appeared in a speech he gave in 1961 at a Philadelphia Yearly Meeting of Quakers. He was explaining to them why he had left the church during the late 1920's and early 1930's. He recalled that the Left then "had a vision, the dream, of a classless and warless world, as the hackneyed phrase goes. This also was a strong factor in making me feel that here, in a sense, was the true church. Here was the fellowship drawn together and drawn forward by the Judaeo-Christian prophetic vision of a 'new earth in which righteousness dwelleth.' The now generally despised Christian liberals had had this vision. As neo-orthodoxy took over, that vision was scorned as naïve and utopian. The 'Kingdom' was something to be realized 'beyond history.' And again, the Communists are those who are today able to convince vast multitudes that they do cherish the ancient dream of brotherhood realized on earth and have the determination to make it come true. This is a measure of the fall of what is called the Free World. The liberal Christians were never, in my opinion, wrong in cherishing their vision. Their mistake, and in a sense, their crime, was not to see that it was revolutionary in character and demanded revolutionary living and action of those who claimed to be its votaries.''

16

THE
JUGGLER

*"He Can Separate What He Wants to See
from What Actually Does Exist."*

AMONG SOME of his colleagues, the most frequent criticism of A. J. Muste's own "revolutionary living and action" has been that he tries to sustain too many projects and committees simultaneously. "He's like a juggler," says Dave Dellinger, "with a hundred balls in the air. When some start to hit the ground, he runs over to catch them, and although he is a marvelous juggler, he can't always catch them all. Besides, being a politician, there are times when he may decide to just let one drop."

"A.J. feels," explains Jim Peck, "that the more valid actions for peace there are, the better. If one attempt fails, he'll just try another." "Part of the drive that keeps A.J. moving from one group to another," adds David McReynolds of the War Registers League, "is that he keeps hoping each new committee will be radical enough by his standards, that it will be able to make a thorough judgment on our whole system. But so far, he hasn't found that one definitively radical stopping place."

Muste has also been charged with seldom excluding anyone from his various contingents. "That man," a co-worker once said of a prospective volunteer, "is more of a screwball than he is a pacifist. Why not leave him out, A.J.?" Muste shook his head negatively. "Well, if what we believe isn't strong enough to absorb *all* these people, it's not entirely real, is it?"

Muste admits that he does become involved in too many projects. "For one thing, I find it difficult to say no, especially to younger people. Too many alleged leaders are overly negative to the young. If young people come to me with an idea, I tend to give it a ride. Also, there are times when I don't really have the right to refuse the use of my name and time. After so many years, one develops a certain prestige. When the cause is a good one, I figure I ought to be involved with it because my name will bring others along."

At one peace meeting in early 1963, Muste was chastised by a young man in the audience for never having joined the Socialist Party. Muste pointed out that he had, in fact, once been a member. Muste grinned. "Anyone is on very dangerous ground," he told the youngster, "when he suggests there is something I haven't joined at one time or another."

Until the end of 1961, one of the roles in which Muste had functioned with particular zest had been as Chief Missioner for the Church Peace Mission. The Mission was first organized in 1950 when the Fellowship of Reconciliation took the initiative in contacting several of those church groups which historically have been predisposed to pacifism. The goal was to set up a combined task force to convert other churches to unqualified opposition to war. Among the constituent units are

various Quaker organizations, the Church of the
Brethren Service Committee, and peace fellowships
from the Baptist, Episcopalian, Unitarian-Universalist,
Lutheran, Methodist, and Presbyterian churches.

The Church Peace Mission issues publications, pro-
motes debates, holds conferences, and has been steadily
growing in influence among theologians and other
churchmen. Its example has helped start a similar movement in Europe. In April, 1962, Muste was gratified
when the Mission was able to distribute a 3,000-word
statement—"A Christian Approach to Nuclear War"—
which more than five hundred ministers and laymen
had signed. The basic text had been prepared some two
years earlier and was the fruition of Muste's work among
churchmen.

After calling on Christians to advocate that the
American government commit itself "to the most serious and unremitting effort to achieve controlled mul-
tilateral disarmament among nations," the signers went
much further than most other religious workers for
peace have been willing to go.

"As Christians," they stated, "we affirm that we cannot under any circumstances sanction the use of nuclear
and other mass-destructive weapons, nor can we sanction
using the threat of massive retaliation by these weapons
for so-called deterrence. We plead with the leaders of
our Government not to persist in piling up nuclear arms
even if other nations are not prepared to agree to the
same course, but to formulate and call on our people to
support a program of unilateral withdrawal from the
nuclear arms race. . . . We urge upon our fellow Christians and upon governmental agencies and educational
leaders serious study of the possibilities of nonviolent
resistance to possible aggression and injustice.

"We call," the statement concluded, "upon the Christian Church to disabuse the American people of the notion widely held that Christian values can be defended and Our Lord and His teaching somehow vindicated by the extermination of Communists. We plead with our fellow Christians to help in carrying out our primary Christian task of winning adherents of communism to Christ by the preaching of His Gospel and the daily practice of the ministry of reconciliation which He has entrusted to us."

Among the signers were Martin Luther King; George A. Buttrick, former preacher to Harvard University; John Haynes Holmes, Minister Emeritus of the Community Church in New York; Clarence E. Pickett, Secretary Emeritus of the Society of Friends; and Walter G. Muelder, Dean of Boston University School of Theology.

Muste, of course, will not consider the Church Peace Mission accomplished until many more thousand religious figures in American life subscribe to and act on these principles. "We have no right to say," he asserts, "that the American people are incapable of moral revulsion against the idea of mass murder of another people when we will not even try to bring the issue before them. Instead we begin with the despairing and insulting assumption that nothing will turn their stomachs. It seems to me that there is a grave challenge here to those Christian theologians who in growing numbers declare in private papers or journals and books with limited circulation that the nation may never *use* the weapons of mass destruction but who do not draw the conclusion that this is academic verbiage and not a moral deliverance unless the production of these weapons is stopped *now* and unless the government and the masses are incessantly told by Christian teachers that the use and hence the production of these weapons is forbidden by the Law and the Gospel."

Muste's insistent attempts to convert the churches to pacifism reflect another area of his conflict with neo-orthodox Christian philosophy. "Theologically," Muste notes, "our purpose is to combat the antipacifism of the 'neo-orthodox' theologians such as Reinhold Niebuhr. Niebuhr was a pacifist in his youth but came to believe that pacifism was naïve. For fear of being thought ingenuous, he took what he considers a 'realistic' position in this hard-boiled world."

Muste has carried the debate to Niebuhr in church and lay journals for many years. In one essay in *Fellowship* magazine a few years ago, Muste charged that "Niebuhr's philosophy was too one-sided and schematic to be truly 'realistic' and now, in the field of the nuclear power struggle, it is irrelevant. It may, indeed, even contribute to the tragic denouement of western civilization, or simply civilization, which political realism sought to avoid."

Muste quoted Niebuhr as having asserted: "It is argued rightly that if we use these instruments we will annihilate ourselves not only physically but morally. If the bomb were ever used, I hope it would kill me, because the moral situation would be something that I could not contemplate. At the same time you cannot disavow its use prematurely without bowing yourself out of responsibility for the whole generation."

"Does Niebuhr mean," Muste asked, "that if the bomb were used, he would have annihilated himself morally? That he would have been implicated in an ultimate moral transgression? If so, then how is it a lesser evil not to disavow now an act that would mean annihilating oneself morally? Instead of being apprehensive that disapproval might be premature, one would surely dread that it might already be too late. . . .

"Nor," Muste continued, "can the argument of the 'lesser evil' be introduced here in the form that a Communist nation might subdue us or even bomb us, for if Niebuhr means what he seems to mean if the bomb is used, then using it *is* the ultimate evil. . . . Neo-orthodox philosophy, by divorcing social ethics from the Kingdom of God, has . . . emasculated the ancient prophetic vision of 'a new heaven and *a new earth,* wherein righteousness dwelleth' and man shall 'learn war no more.' Instead it has tended to serve to desensitize the national conscience to war at the very time when war technology broke through all restraints."

Niebuhr insists that "pacifism was irrelevant in dealing with Hitler. That's why I broke with it then, and it's unrealistic now. It's not enough to say that things are wrong. You have to deal with actual power structures, and as mixed as the motives of an individual are, the motives of a nation are even more ambiguous. Preaching love to them won't bring peace. I will say that unlike many pacifists, Muste is not personally bitter or self-righteous, but he is certainly guileless."

Muste continues on the attack. "If Christian churches," he has summarized the basis of his differences with Niebuhr in *Liberation,* "were . . . to serve as critics of the power-state and as revolutionizing leaven within the culture—as Negro churches of the South are doing in the race struggle at the moment—instead of being identified with and therefore bulwarks of the state and the culture, how different the political situation might be. What new possibilities of international reconciliation might emerge! . . . Reinhold Niebuhr's theology has paradoxically led him to the point where politically he is unable to break out of the context of the power

structure and recognize . . . that a realistic dealing with
the present crisis is possible only if it is now recognized
that Christian or ethical insights and values are no
longer politically irrelevant. Though he recognizes love
as a sort of ultimate, in practice he does not accept
Martin Buber's counsel that, difficult as it may be, our
task is precisely to 'drive the plowshare of the norma-
tive principle'—i.e. love—into the hard soil of political
fact."

Although Muste and Niebuhr have remained on
friendly terms through the years, their exchanges occasionally become tart. In 1948, when Muste opposed the
Marshall Plan, Niebuhr wrote him, "You say the United
States is trying to 'corner the whole of Europe ideologi-
cally and politically.' I might say that you are trying to
corner the whole of Christianity for pacifism." Niebuhr
added that "the cause of democracy is not pure and this
is partly a contest of power, but that is always true in
politics. If you want a pure contest of ideas, you will
have to leave the world."

In the past few years, although Niebuhr has not declared for unilateral disarmament, his reaction to the
deterrence concept seems to Muste to be coming closer
to his own. Muste cites Niebuhr's preface to the pamphlet, *Community of Fear*, issued in October, 1960, by
the Center for the Study of Democratic Institutions,
established by the Fund for the Republic. Niebuhr
writes that "ultimately the ever accelerated pace of the
arms race must lead to disaster, even if neither side consciously desires the ultimate war. That is why the old
slogans of 'bargaining from strength' and 'deterring attack by the prospect of massive retaliation' have become
irrelevant. A fresh approach is needed."

In one of his persistent efforts to help set up the kind
of communication which might stimulate fresh ap-

proaches, Muste became involved with the Committees of Correspondence (later changed to Council for Correspondence). The group was organized at a Bear Mountain, New York, meeting in March, 1960, with a Coordinating Committee including, among others, David Riesman, Robert Gilmore, H. Stuart Hughes, and Muste. The intent of the organization has been to persuade the intellectual community that the concept of stockpiling arms as a deterrent to war must be radically reappraised.

"We call," said the original Bear Mountain statement, "for unilateral steps toward disarmament both on principle and as a practical strategy, which represents neither surrender to Communism nor wishful fantasy, since no country courageous and rational enough to thus disarm would be an easy victory for any form of dictatorship. We risk a great deal in reliance on nuclear arms: we must be willing to take risks in pursuit of peace." The Council issues a monthly newsletter with such contributors as H. Stuart Hughes, David Riesman, and Nathan Glazer. Although the circulation is small, the publication has succeeded in provoking debate and some degree of experimental thinking on the problem of finding workable alternatives to peace-through-armament.

A. J. Muste himself has long been a Council for Correspondence on his own. He not only deals with a huge amount of regular mail in connection with his various committees and projects; but when in his reading he finds signs of protest against war or social injustice, Muste often makes a point of encouraging the author.

Phillips Moulton, President of Wesley College in North Dakota, wrote an article some twenty years ago on "The Church and Labor" in a very small journal, *Economic Justice*. Moulton recalls: "I hardly expected anyone to notice it, but A.J. took the time to write a note of praise and appreciation. Later, when I was a pastor in Brooklyn, a reporter for the *New York Herald Tribune* quoted some rather strong statements I had made about the failure of the church to witness adequately against war. Again I received a congratulatory note from A.J. I don't know if peace will be achieved, but if it is, it shall not be brought about by the average run of college presidents or bishops but by men like A.J. who hear many conflicting voices, but only attend to that which rings true. It's an inspiration just to think about the old goat."

Professor Victor Paschkis, Professor of Mechanical Engineering at Columbia University, also tells of hearing unexpectedly from Muste. In August, 1947, Paschkis had written an article for a Quaker periodical pointing out that those scientists who were trying to collect funds to educate the public about the dangers of atomic weapons were simultaneously continuing their work on those weapons. Muste telephoned Pachkis a couple of days after the article had appeared, and suggested that there must be other scientists who were thinking along the same lines. He provided Pachkis with several names, and in a sense stimulated the Columbia University professor to start two years later the Society for Social Responsibility in Science.

The Society's purpose "is to induce scientists to recognize a personal responsibility for the anticipated consequences to society of their work and to always exercise their profession for the benefit of humanity." In addition to a newsletter and the holding of meetings, the Society provides an employment service that is "available to any scientist who has job problems related to conscience or to the use of his professional skill for constructive purposes." In fourteen years, the Society has grown from a charter group of some thirty Americans to over seven hundred scientists in twenty countries throughout the world. Among its members have been six Nobel prize winners, including the late Albert Einstein.

"Up to 1700," Paschkis has explained in a *New York Post* interview, "it was commonly accepted that scientists were responsible for the social implications of their work. The breakdown came when, during the argument between the fundamentalists and scientists in England, the Royal Society, which was then being formed, said in effect that we will not be embroiled in this, we will draw no connection between science and morality. Today we are slowly coming back to the idea that we must." It is the viewpoint of Paschkis and his colleagues in the Society for Social Responsibility in Science that each scientist must first answer to himself as to whether he can work on military projects with a clear conscience. If he cannot, he should decline all such work and should be supported in that refusal.

To Muste's satisfaction, the Society has called "for an unwavering search for alternatives" to war or the threat of war. It is also working toward establishing a kind of commitment pledge for all scientists in which they would agree not to engage in destructive work.

In his communications with Muste, Victor Paschkis has been impressed by Muste's logical analysis of power politics and the pragmatism of his strategy against war. "So many of those working in the peace movements," Paschkis observes, "are fuzzy, but A.J. is unusually keen. He can separate what he wants to see from what actually does exist. Accordingly, he doesn't take the easy route and work only among the converted and the nearly converted. He doesn't lose contact with the power structure although he opposes it. He tries to reach Congressmen, and he writes letters to the general press and occasional articles for the nonpacifist magazines. A.J. reaches more varieties of people with his message than any other pacifist."

17

RELIGION, IRRELIGION, AND NONVIOLENCE

"Some Atheists Are Closer to What I Mean by Religion Than a Good Many Regular Churchgoers Who Use 'Religious' Language."

A FREQUENT obstacle encountered by Muste in his quest for converts to pacifism is the view that absolute pacifism requires religious faith. Norman Thomas, for example, has joined with Muste in many statements and demonstrations against nuclear testing, but he does not consider himself a pacifist in Muste's sense. He says rather wistfully, "I once was a pacifist, and I was happier when I was. But my belief was based on a conviction that if we did certain things in line with God's will and the teachings of Jesus, God would certainly take care of the rest. I now think that I am forced to consider the alternatives, since the world isn't that much in God's hands."

Muste disagrees that pacifism necessarily requires a corollary religious belief. "I know atheists in the movement who are religious in the very real sense that they are committed to pacifism, not as a technique, but as a way of life. Take a man like Bertrand Russell who is not 'religious' in the sense in which the term is usually used. He's living his life according to more than materialistic precepts. Religion, after all, implies an individual's commitment to something beyond himself. It need not have anything to do with institutionalized churches and dogma.

"Some atheists, in fact, are closer to what I mean by religion than a good many regular churchgoers who use 'religious' language. These atheists might resent being called religious, but fundamentally they're Christian. The fact that a person does not verbalize his basic orientation in Christian theological terms and does not use Christian symbolism to express his sense of identification with and basic love for human beings does not mean to me that he does not live as a Christian in the basic meaning of that term. There are, on the other hand, many people who regard themselves as Christian but are not pacifists and who therefore are not in that respect living an entirely Christian existence."

Muste's own concept of God is mystical. "I have a feeling of awe in the presence of the universe. Physically, I find myself part of a total reality which I did not create and which, in a very real sense, did create me. I have to maintain some kind of relationship to this universe, and I say 'God' to describe my conviction that man is not the highest or the ultimate being, that there is something beyond ourselves. I don't like the terms 'force,' 'evolution' or 'history' in this sense, because they make this reality outside ourselves too depersonalized. Nor do I conceive of an anthropomorphic God. Essentially, however, as real as the concept of God is to me, God is undefinable. You can only talk about Him in the language of symbolism and poetry. When you try to define God, you are thinking of Him as one object among other objects, and that is exactly what God is not.

"The experience of God is an openness to all experience, but my religious belief can never be *contrary* to reason, and so I cannot accept such dogmas as the Virgin Birth. Yet my belief is not *limited* to reason. My point is that the intellect cannot fully define all of experience, and there is, therefore, something more than intellect and its products in the total reality of my existence. Part of that 'something more' is a recognition of the moral imperative to be honest and loving with regard to all other human beings. For me, the acceptance of that moral imperative is a yielding, if you wish, to the will of God."

As for immortality, Muste says that "the idea of an extension of the individual personality after death or the attempt to conceive of a physical resurrection of the self is intellectually untenable for me. On the other hand, I don't believe that death is an absolute ending. There is a quality in human existence of living in eternity, of living beyond oneself. I could say I believe that there is a continuation after death of one's effects on others but that again is an attempt to rationalize. Where I come out ultimately is that you cannot rest on a purely rationalistic view of life. There is a quality to experience that is irrational and spontaneous and that cannot be definitively described or exhausted by the intellect. That's the best I can do in indicating what I mean by God."

Muste seldom attends church. "I haven't gone regularly since the last war. My wife couldn't attend services because of her health, and so I spent Sundays with her. Now, I go only on special occasions such as Armistice Day, or when there are services for peace. Formal services are not important to me, and some varieties would be very unpleasant. Also, I don't think I ever believed in the efficacy of petitionary prayer. I tend to regard all such forms of prayer as bordering on magic. To me prayer is essentially an emotion of the spirit in which you open yourself to God, the spirit of love and the universe."

Although pacifism is now a basic tenet of Muste's religious beliefs, in his early training in the Dutch Reformed Church, he did not, as he says, "get so much as a hint that there was such a possibility as a pacifist interpretation of the Gospel. Before the First War, it was Tolstoy who began to influence me toward nonviolence, as he did many pacifists of my generation. I must have talked about him when I was just starting in the ministry, because the first present ever given me by parishioners—it was the congregation of the Fort Washington Collegiate Church in New York—was a collection of Tolstoy's works on religious and philosophical themes. Then my own decision for pacifism came during the First War, and at that time I became a Quaker.

"By the time of the Lawrence strike in 1919, I was already interested in the techniques of nonviolent direct action as part of pacifism. Those of us pacifists involved in the strike had heard of Gandhi in a general way, but he was not yet the influence in the West that he became later. I certainly hadn't studied Gandhi's methods at that time. During my years at Brookwood and in labor organizing, I continued to educate workers to develop nonviolent techniques as a pragmatic counteroffensive to the strong-arm squads of management. I knew that if we used force we'd be playing into management's hands. It wasn't until I left the Trotskyites, however, that I really began studying Gandhi. For me the most important book on his techniques was *War Without Violence* by Krishnalal Shridharani, published by Harcourt, Brace in 1939. I wrote and talked about it and was influential in getting other American pacifists to read it.

"Shridharani himself was in the United States at the time, and I came to know him. He was uninterested in the typical Western pacifism of personal witness, and was even rather contemptuous of it. He felt that you had to fight for your beliefs, although with nonviolent techniques. His actionist philosophy impressed me, as did the fact that his book was a sociological and political study of Gandhi's movement, not just an inspirational tract. It was in line with my own long-term conviction that pacifism had to be related to social and political realities.

"I never met Gandhi himself, but we did have some correspondence. I don't regret not having known him, because I never felt about anyone that I absolutely had to see him to understand his ideas. I think, in fact, that there has been too much of a tendency among some Indians and pacifists elsewhere to worship Gandhi."

Muste, in any case, was more interested in adapting Gandhi's ideas to the American situation. "The main thing Gandhi did for me was not so much in terms of teaching me special techniques—because I'd already worked out many of those—but in giving me inspiration through his successful application of nonviolent action in a large-scale political situation. I knew by 1936 that I could no longer apply the techniques of Lenin and Trotsky because they violated my personal convictions. Watching Gandhi achieve political ends in a way with which I could agree was enormously encouraging. Historically, it became clear that it was Gandhi who confronted Lenin in this era."

Muste also found support for his concept of nonpassive pacifism in Christ. "Truly," Muste once wrote for *Fellowship,* "he renounced violence and demanded the revolution in the heart. But he would not have been crucified for that, if he had been 'passive' about the ecclesiastical hierarchy of his day and its narrow Sabbatarianism, and about people who 'devour widow's houses' and make long prayers in public, and if he had paid taxes and if he had not cleansed the Temple and made that entry into Jerusalem as King—albeit a new kind of King—of the Jews. It is really not possible to be for something in this world without being against something else."

Muste's insistent advocacy of nonviolence for all those who want to change the world has occasionally led skeptics to challenge him with hypothetical dilemmas. "Suppose," he was asked recently, "someone was being attacked in your presence. Would you not intervene?"

"I would not," Muste answered, "take an absolutist position in the sense that I'd simply look on, unless I were physically immobilized. Passivity by itself is not a pacifist attitude, as I understand the term. I would place myself between the attacker and the intended victim and take the blows upon myself. Furthermore, I believe very firmly in what Gandhi often said, that it is better to resist by violence than to be cowardly and fail to intervene. A person who resists evil—even violently—is in a better moral position than someone who sees an evil and, for whatever reason, keeps still.

"But," Muste added, "if there is in a given situation someone who is at peace with himself and who has an attitude of love toward everyone in that situation, a quality which Gandhi calls 'soul force' *does* operate. I don't mean nonviolent resistance might not fail. But violence also fails frequently, and in general I think the law that violence begets violence and fear begets fear comes near to being an operational absolute. I can't think of a situation in which falling back on violence as a means of defense would not produce more violence.

"I'm convinced that in many strike situations, for example, the fact that it was known I would not use violence protected other people with me as well as myself from physical abuse. In the aftermath of the shootings in Marion, North Carolina, in 1929, and in two or three mining situations in West Virginia in 1931 and 1932, I was told later that hired goons had come to our meetings to create a disturbance and, among other things, to kill me. They went back to their employers and said they couldn't do it because it was clear that when it came to a showdown, we would not resist."

"That's all very well on a personal level," Muste's questioner persisted, "but what about Hitler and the Jews? Would nonviolent resistance have done the Jews any good?"

"War in itself," Muste answered, "makes all manner of atrocities more possible and more severe. In this country, it was the war that made possible our confining of innocent Japanese in concentration camps. As for the mass murders of the Jews, I do not believe that our entering the war saved many Jews. The war, in fact, made it easier for Hitler to carry out his policies toward the Jews to their fullest extent. He was able to play on the fact that the Germans felt their country to be beleaguered.

"It would, of course, have been before war was declared," Muste continued, "that nonviolence might have been most effective. The situation could have been a very different one if the Jewish community in Germany had had any concept at all of nonviolent resistance in a situation of that kind. A very few did, but, in the community as a whole, there were those who at first tried to maintain their positions and to compromise with the situation. Others tried to ignore what has happening as long as they could. And others felt impotent.

"Yet," Muste said, "if even a significant minority of the Jews had attempted nonviolent resistance, that action would have gone a long distance toward causing a lot of non-Jewish Germans to change their own attitudes toward the Jews. Before the war, I was shocked at the extent of anti-Semitism among Germans in the churches, including some church leaders. I mean among people who took Christianity seriously, as well as those who were nominal or non-churchgoers.

"If, in the face of Hitler," says Muste, "a considerable number of Jews had tried to react according to the higher principles of the Old Testament—not "an eye for an eye and a tooth for a tooth" but rather "in returning and rest shall ye be saved; in quietness and confidence shall be your strength"—this would have had a profound effect on many sections of the German population. Such a reaction might have made it much more difficult for Hitler to have attained the kind of total control he later did achieve.

"Nonviolence by the Jews," Muste added, "before and after war had begun, could have had another result. It is a fact that there were important elements in German life, including the army, which were hostile to Hitler and eventually engaged in conspiracies to assassinate him. The general attitude of the Allied Powers toward these people was extremely skeptical, and their existence did not affect the Allied commitment to unconditional surrender. I think it is arguable that if there had been some degree of mass nonviolent resistance by the Jews inside Germany, the Allies might have been more impressed by the possibilities of utilizing anti-Hitler forces inside Germany rather than concentrating wholly on the military approach."

"But did there not come a time," Muste's questioner went on, "when nonviolent resistance under Hitler could have had no effect whatsoever?"

"My answer," Muste replied, "depends on what is meant by the question. If you ask whether the Jews by that time were in a position to do anything at all to help themselves, the answer would be an almost unconditional 'no.' There had been no preparation for nonviolence; they were trapped. If the question, however, supposes that there were leaders among the Jews who grasped the situation in terms of a redemptive act by the Jewish community, then the extermination of so many Jews might have had a different result. In that case, instead of accepting destruction because there was no alternative to submission, these leaders could have said, 'Let us nonviolently refuse to cooperate with this regime at every point we can. Let us, in whatever ways are still open to us, appeal in this way to all Germans to deliver themselves from this regime and from war.' The Jews, in that event, would have been *choosing* martyrdom, not allowing it to be inflicted upon them. That martyrdom would have been a witness and an act for the redemption of the German people.

"If," Muste continued, "there had been such leaders and if people had gathered around them, this would have been a crucial event in human history. It might even have been a turning point in that whole drive toward violence which Camus talks about in *Neither Victims Nor Executioners*. On the other hand, what actually did happen has served to confirm the idea that in the last analysis, you can only meet violence with violence. The experience of the Jews under Hitler has provided no escape from that very vicious circle which brought the German people, including their Jewish victims, into war and destruction, and which continues today.

"There *were* pacifists, you know," Muste emphasized, "in Germany and elsewhere in Europe throughout the war. They refused to support the Nazis in any way; and particularly in Denmark and Norway, they organized very effective nonviolent resistance campaigns. Wherever they were in Europe, these pacifists saved as many Jews as they could. Some of the wartime pacifists survived; some perished. Invariably, they won the respect of the people in their communities.

"I remember in 1947, during my first postwar trip to Europe, I attended a conference in a French town at the Swiss border, Le Chambon. A couple of F.O.R. people had founded a school there and had kept it going during the war. They sheltered Jews in the school, and helped more than a hundred over the border into Switzerland.

"At that meeting, there were a number of young men who had been *maquis* and had resisted the occupation forces violently. They were still not pacifists, but I noticed that they treated the pacifists with very great respect, a reaction that was opposite to what one might have expected. I asked several of the *maquis* why they felt so warmly toward the pacifists. 'How do you think,' one of them answered, 'we learned it was possible for a people to resist after the Nazis came? At first, when the Germans arrived, they released pacifists who were in jail. "Well," we thought, "naturally, they would. Pacifists, in a sense, are their friends." But the pacifists continued to refuse to obey German orders. They kept on helping the Jews, and would not salute German officers. We learned from their example that we didn't have to lose our souls. We did not adopt their techniques, to be sure, but we were not mature enough then to devise nonviolent ways of resistance.' "

For himself, Muste has synthesized Christianity and absolute pacifism into a thoroughly consistent personal philosophy. Perhaps the most distilled explanation of that philosophy he has ever made was in the course of a 1961 Muste speech at a Philadelphia Meeting of Quakers. The essence of that speech was published in the pamphlet, *Saints for This Age* (Pendle Hill Pamphlets, Wallingford, Pennsylvania).

Muste's text was the opening of the Apostle Paul's Letter to the Romans: "To all that be in Rome, beloved of God, called to be saints." Muste pointed out that the last four words "did not mean that they were all or always extremely virtuous, ascetic, saintly in the usual sense of the word. Paul's Letter to the Corinthians suggests that there was quite a variety of saints, not all saintly.

"What is clear," Muste underlined, "is that they got a great kick out of being saints, that is, Christians. Joy was an outstanding characteristic of them. On the face of it, you cannot command Christians to be joyous, as if it were a duty. But the Apostle could perpetuate the paradox and shout: '*Rejoice,* and again I say, Rejoice.' It was simply inconceivable that the experience of fellowship with one another and with Christ should not produce effervescence. Personally, I always have a certain suspicion of alleged saintliness which lacks this tone of buoyancy and effervescence."

Muste then focused on the direction this quality of Christianity took: "Saintliness expressed itself in *experimentation,* growing out of and demanded by the experience of love and of release, of having cut loose. Experimentation took place in relation to violence: the early Christians did not serve in Caesar's armies—'Our

Lord is disarming, Peter disarmed every soldier.' It took place in economic life, in a religious communism of consumption, though not of production. Such experimentation seemed to follow naturally from their altered view of the nature of history."

Toward the end of the speech, Muste elaborated on what he had meant in speaking of the early Christians as "having cut loose." They understood, he noted, "that for all its size, seeming stability and power, the 'world,' the 'age,' in which they lived was ephemeral, weak, doomed. It was not built on sound foundations. They had, therefore, turned their backs on it in the sense that they were not placing their bets on it, did not give it their ultimate allegiance, were not intimidated by what it could do to them, and did not seek satisfaction and security within its structure, under its standards."

Bringing this kind of Christian approach to the present, Muste continued: "There is no doubt that our world is doomed. I do not mean by this that I think nuclear war and resultant nuclear annihilation are inevitable. It would be even more risky, I think, to assert that they will not happen. But I am not here making a political judgment or calculation. In a much profounder sense, the world we have known is passing. The uncovering of nuclear secrets, other developments we might mention, make this certain. Mankind *has* to find the way into a radically new world. Mankind has to become a 'new humanity' or perish."

After a trip to India in late 1962, Muste elaborated on his conception of the way to "a radically new world." The world, he emphasized, "needs a revolution in feeling, in sensitivity, in orientation, in the spirit of man. This is an age in which the world of the physicist has become one of virtually infinite possibility. In every world of research, the walls are down. In the realm of human relations, however, of politics in the basic sense, no such breakthrough has occurred. Here the walls press in upon man. The operative phrase is 'the politically possible,' which means what is possible within the existing sociopolitical context, the prevailing frame of thought. It would, in fact, be more accurate to say the outmoded, rapidly vanishing, pre-nuclear-age context and frame of thought. As Einstein stated it definitively a decade and a half ago: 'The splitting of the atom has changed everything save our modes of thinking, and thus we drift toward unparalleled catastrophe.' "

18

RECRUITING
NEGATIVE
POWER

*"It Is an Absolute Power—the Only Power
That Cannot Corrupt Those Who Exercise
It."*

IN HIS speech to the Quakers in Philadelphia, Muste,
after having described the "experimentation" of the
early Christians as an inevitable result of the nature of
their faith, looked at his audience and added: "It is
surely in this context very significant how many Friends
experienced a refreshing, a nourishing of the inner life
of the Spirit when recently a thousand of them 'cut
loose' and 'experimented,' standing in silent vigil around
the Pentagon."

Such vigils—and all the more active demonstrations
for peace—are regarded by Muste as increasingly vital
for pacifists, absolute and nuclear, to undertake. "To
be effective," he observes often, "those who work for
peace must remember that one major reason previous
peace efforts have failed to register is that military and
political leaders know that the overwhelming majority
of people who take part in those campaigns will con-

sent to be conscripted again whenever they are called upon. Politicians are not so dumb as not to realize that such paper votes and resolutions can be largely discounted. What is needed is *active* refusal to support violence under *all* conditions. 'Negative power' is what Herbert Read calls this elementary power to refuse to slaughter. 'It is in the hands of youth,' he says, 'and it is an absolute power—the only power that cannot corrupt those who exercise it.' "

During the summer and fall of 1960, Muste helped young members of the Committee for Nonviolent Action exercise their "negative power" in an extended Polaris Action project. The Committee set up an office in New London, Connecticut, where the United States Submarine Base and General Dynamics Corporation's Electric Boats shipyards are located. Work was being completed on outfitting submarines with massively destructive weapons, Polaris missiles, which now have a range of 2,500 miles and can carry an H-bomb warhead thirty times more powerful than the Hiroshima bomb. The Committee conducted walks, vigils, passed out leaflets, and tried without notable success to convince workers at the shipyards that they were engaged in egregiously inhuman pursuits. On several occasions, C.N.V.A. members boarded Polaris submarines as a protest action, and were promptly hauled off.

By October, 1960, every window in the New London C.N.V.A. office had been broken, and several Committee members had been physically attacked. The pacifists, however, refused to be provoked to retaliatory violence and continued demonstrating. Gradually, a few members of the community came to the battered office to learn more about Polaris Action; and publicity for the demonstrations pyramided in the press and finally included national television. As usual, Muste had acted as the major buffer between the young agitators and the local ministry, police, and courts.

Another elderly radical pacifist involved in Polaris Action was Ammon Hennacy of the *Catholic Worker*. Hennacy, an anarchist, has been associated with Muste in several projects over the years. While he respects Muste's integrity, Hennacy speaks of Muste as "a left-wing pacifist and a right-wing radical. Actually, there aren't any radicals anymore. They've all become politicians." Hennacy has been jailed more often than Muste, has been refusing to pay taxes since 1943, and each year he pickets the Internal Revenue Service at tax time. Hennacy, in fact, is the most indefatigable placard-carrier in the movement, preferring continual alfresco demonstrating to Muste's occasional involvement with politics.

A slight, wiry man of vast energy and irrepressible determination, Hennacy was carrying a sign during one attack by New London townspeople on the C.N.V.A. demonstrators. An infuriated shipyard worker snatched Hennacy's placard from his hand. Hennacy fixed his icy blue eyes on the offender and said sternly, "God bless you." The worker returned the sign.

Muste feels that projects such as Polaris Action, including the implacable witnessing of such warriors for peace as Ammon Hennacy, have considerable cumulative value. "Over a period of time," Muste has explained, "people in the community do become interested and troubled. During Polaris Action, for example, in a half-dozen of the leading churches in New London and nearby Groton, groups of young people, including Navy families, invited C.N.V.A. members to talk to them about the philosophy of nonviolence and the arguments for unilateral disarmament. And I was asked to speak at a vesper service at the Connecticut College for

Women. The chaplain at the college is not a pacifist, but he and others there did want the faculty and the girls to know more about Polaris Action. I was invited, by the way, at a time when the college was trying to raise money for new buildings and hoped to get some of it from General Dynamics. Also I believe there is some value even in the fact that members of the community do get angry with us. I would rather they were furious than apathetic."

The year before, Muste had been in Africa, trying to inculcate the concept of "negative power" there by his presence on the Sahara Protest team demonstrating against French nuclear testing on that continent. When Muste left for Africa toward the end of 1959 to lecture on nonviolent techniques and to help coordinate the Sahara Protest team, several friends of his thought the mission farcical. "It was downright silly," Roger Baldwin said, "for Americans to organize Africans on nonviolent lines." Muste's answer was that "it may well have seemed silly, but African leaders told us that our very presence was a great encouragement to them. They no longer felt alone in their opposition to making their continent another nuclear testing ground."

In the spring of 1960, the government of Ghana, in association with Morocco and several other independent African states, initiated a Positive Action Conference for Peace and Security in Africa. The conference took place in Ghana, and Muste came as a delegate of the Committee for Nonviolent Action. Prime Minister Kwame Nkrumah addressed the delegates. Hardly an apostle himself of Muste's kind of nonviolence in his domestic conflicts, Nkrumah did support this form of nonviolent foreign policy, and he proposed future mass nonviolent attempts to march into the testing areas.

The Prime Minister noted that the original team,

with which Muste had traveled through Ghana, had
been turned back at the Upper Volta border. He added,
however, that "it would not matter if not a single person ever reached the site, for the effect of hundreds of
people from every corner of Africa and from outside it
crossing the artificial barriers that divide Africa to risk
imprisonment and arrest would be a protest that the
people of France (with the exception of the De Gaulle
Government), and the world could not ignore."

Dr. Darrell Randall, then Associate Executive Director of the National Council of the Churches of Christ,
observed at the time that "Muste's presence on the team
really did a great deal for American public relations in
Africa. Here was a man, a very quiet but forceful American, who had come out of a concern for *them* and was
willing to risk his own safety in working with Africans."

"It was extraordinarily hot all the time A.J. was
there," according to Bayard Rustin, another member of
the team. "I was fearful for him the first couple of days,
but he quickly adjusted to the climate and plunged
into a rigorous schedule that left him little sleep, and
on which he thrived."

Like the other members of the Sahara Protest team,
Muste usually began work in Accra by six in the morning, before the heat became oppressive. "He was used
to rising later," says Reverend Michael Scott of Britain,
one of the leaders of the team, "but he didn't at all
complain at our hours, although I must admit he was
grateful for the tea I brought him each morning when
he awoke. All he did seem to become exercised about
was his hat. He was looking for a particular quality of
Panama hat and searched through many, long hot streets
in the markets of Accra before he was satisfied. Otherwise, he was quite content with working conditions. He
was a great help to us because of the boldness and clarity

of his thinking. He also had an important steadying
effect, especially in a situation like the one we faced.
Our team was quite mixed, and many of its members
differed widely in their motivations and expectations.
There was much potential danger in the situation, and
A.J.'s internal strength of purpose and his ability to
communicate clearly did much to keep the team from
losing its bearings. He never pales at the most difficult
and unexpected complications, and he never stops working."

Wherever Muste travels, he drives himself as relentlessly as he does at home. He also sends back long reports
on his findings to American pacifist magazines and to his
mailing list. On the other hand, Muste devotes considerable time back in New York to reporting on the
American peace movement for pacifist publications
abroad. He is also often consulted by radical pacifist
leaders in other countries. Hugh Brock, editor of *Peace
News,* a brisk, realistic international weekly published
in London, has pointed out that "A.J. has served the
British pacifist movement well by interpreting for us
many of the radical trends in America which would
not normally get known on this side of the Atlantic.
He made us aware of the activities of the Congress of
Racial Equality and the radical American Peacemakers
Group. It was the example of the Peacemakers which encouraged the formation in Britain in 1952 of the Nonviolent Resistance Group here. The experience of the
Peacemakers in nonviolent direct action helped make
possible the first Aldermaston March here and provided
the radical cutting edge to our campaign for Nuclear
Disarmament."

The Peacemakers group was formed in America in
1948 as a result of a conference of radical pacifists that
Muste was instrumental in arranging. He was secretary

from 1948-53, and left the next year. "His interest
waned," says Ernest Bromley, who edits *The Peacemaker,* the group's journal, "as he became more interested again in working with groups politically. He
stopped coming to our conferences, but he has continued his individual witness on nonpayment of taxes."

A longtime radical pacifist with ties to both Muste
and the Peacemakers has a more detailed explanation
for Muste's departure from the group. "In the first place,
the Peacemakers are centered in Ohio and consist of
a core of forty to fifty of the most radical, thought not
necessarily the most active, pacifists in the country.
They do not accept any kind of leadership or organization discipline in contrast to the radical pacifists centered in New York. The latter are more politically
oriented, more organizable, and are willing to accept
A.J. as their leader. The Ohio group is more anarchistic,
and besides is skeptical of the 'city slickers.' They feel
that the New York pacifists are too involved in gaining
power in the peace movement and also use too many
political stratagems in their direct-action projects. Muste
finally decided that for once he could not reconcile the
irreconcilable, and he preferred to concentrate his energies among the nonanarchists."

Yet most of the Peacemakers continue to feel close
to Muste personally, and respect him. Ernest Bromley's
wife, Marion, was once Muste's secretary in the Fellowship of Reconciliation. "I had become disturbed in
spirit," she recalls about working in industry during
the war, "and had written the F.O.R. asking if they
needed any secretarial help. They answered that A.J.
was losing his secretary, and asked if I were interested.
The salary was about a third of what I was making, and
I wasn't sure one could live in New York on such an
income. I delayed my decision. A few months later,

A.J. spoke in my hometown. He had a slight cold, and was so thin I felt he must surely be nearing the end of his life. I told a close friend that it wasn't going to matter for very long whether he had a secretary or not. That was in 1942.

"When I finally did go to work for him, I was amazed at his capacity for activity. During those years, in addition to keeping the F.O.R. organizationally effective, he kept up a voluminous correspondence with pacifists across the country. He traveled and was in demand as a speaker. In fact, he was equally appealing to children in school assemblies, college groups, F.O.R. meetings, and civic organizations. While he always looked frail, he could speak four times a day, dictate correspondence in between, and travel on to the next town that evening."

Lectures still take up a considerable part of Muste's schedule. Sometimes the audiences are small, although no longer so small as they were in the 1940's and early 1950's before the upsurge of interest in pacifism among ministers and college students. In 1952, for example, Muste came to Philadelphia to address the annual conference of the local F.O.R. chapter, and was faced by only fifteen people. They huddled together among the empty chairs, miserable at having let their important guest down. Muste took the compact audience into a smaller room and set off a long discussion in which everyone participated ardently. "You see," he said at the end of the evening, "a group's size is important qualitatively, not quantitatively." "We had already reached that conclusion," recalls a student who had been in the audience.

Muste has also continued his role as the Pied Piper of the peace movement. Many later full-time workers in such units as the American Friends Service Committee, the F.O.R., and other pacifist organizations remember a Muste visit to their schools as having either awakened their interest in pacifism or confirmed their barely nascent views on the subject. "He has lectured," says Tartt Bell of the American Friends Service Committee, "on literally hundreds of campuses. A big reason he makes so lasting an impression is that intellectually he's usually the peer of anyone on the campus. Often, until A.J. came, students thought of pacifists as vague sentimentalists, and many would come to a Muste debate with the sweet expectancy of watching him get his ears pinned back by some history professor. He always held his own and more, and with such gentleness of spirit as well as analytical power that he couldn't help alter some students' views of pacifism."

Muste rarely meets resistance to his appearances from college authorities, but there was an incident in 1941 when an undergraduate political club at the University of North Carolina invited Muste to speak. After Muste agreed, he was informed by letter that the club's faculty adviser thought Muste's visit might not be wise. Muste sent the letter to Dr. Frank Graham, President of the university at the time. Graham wired Muste to come, met him at the railroad station, attended the meeting, invited Muste to dine at the faculty club, and drove him to his return train.

At times a Muste campus call has led to direct results that might well appall a skittish faculty adviser. Allan Brick, now a college teacher, was a freshman at Haverford in the 1946-47 term when he and two friends were among those who heard Muste tell the college's weekly assembly that the most affirmative gesture a young man could make was to say no to conscription. "Then," says Brick, "we talked with him, just the three of us alone for quite a long stretch. At the end of the summer of 1947, my roommate tore up his draft card and sent it to the Attorney General, while I merely registered as a c.o. I've been atoning for registering ever since."

In the spring of 1959, it was Allan Brick, then at Dartmouth, who presided as Muste addressed a meeting of the Dartmouth Human Rights Society, a new student-faculty group concerned with antimilitarism and civil liberties. Muste had come at a tense time. Throughout the term, there had been conflict on campus about compulsory R.O.T.C. As had happened in several other colleges throughout the country, a movement to abolish the military training program had begun among some Dartmouth undergraduates. Two days before Muste's speech, some two dozen dissenters had marred the symmetry of an R.O.T.C. parade on the college green by appearing with placards carrying distinctly unflattering comments about such military pomp on campus. Their protest had required courage, because there had been rumors that local police were at the ready and that one particularly pugnacious R.O.T.C. officer had commanded his forces to march over the demonstrators. Nobody was trampled, but R.O.T.C. enthusiasts were incensed.

Brick was worried about what might happen to America's number one pacifist in so inflammatory a situation. He had heard that a commando cadre of R.O.T.C. undergraduates planned to attend the lecture to execute revenge. The Navy, moreover, had arranged for its crack drill team to be appointed special deputies to the Hanover town police. These new peace officers were shown how best to apply rifle butts on demonstrators.

Three hundred students came to hear Muste. Shortly after starting time, twenty crew-cut bravoes from the R.O.T.C. entered the hall and slouched together in a phalanx at the rear. Muste began speaking about what he termed the fallacy of America's policy of building nuclear arms to prevent aggression. He continued for ten minutes until the leader of the opposition, a large blond young man in a tiger-striped shirt, erupted in a mocking cheer after Muste had quoted George Kennan's view that a policy related to Christian values should be substituted for the present buildup of retaliatory force. For the next twenty minutes, Muste continued over an obbligato of rather jittery, intermittent jeers from the R.O.T.C. contingent at the rear. Muste, who is more accustomed to hecklers than most night club comics, ignored the static.

The R.O.T.C. delegation soon started rolling marbles down the wooden steps of the aisle, punctuating the tumbrel-like sound of the marbles' descent with further guffaws. Allan Brick sat on the platform, waiting for Muste to show some sign of irritation or distraction. After forty minutes, Muste was still unruffled, and his opponents had subsided. "A.J.," Brick recalls, "continued to communicate passionate intensity to the large majority who were by now quite awed by his success. I've never heard him speak so compellingly as he did at the end of that talk."

Muste sat down and Allan Brick rose. Brick commended Muste's demonstration of "honesty, courage and compassion" (the words Muste himself had used at the close of his speech by way of listing the ingredients of a desirable American foreign policy). The jeers again began, but Brick surprised the demonstrators by asking their leader in the tiger shirt if he could "articulate" a question to Mr. Muste.

The youngster stood up and with no discernible politeness asked Muste if it were not true that he was both a Communist and a coward. Muste calmly told the lad that he had at one time been a Trotskyite, and he explained why he had left the party. As for his alleged cowardice, Muste said that it was hardly within a reasonable definition of cowardice to maintain that reliance on military weapons was not only immoral but now also promised massive destruction of other peoples and suicide for one's own country.

"We are *all* aware," Muste looked directly at the blond boy, "that there are now new, nuclear elements in the concept that arms can be a deterrent to war. I would think that particularly nonpacifists like yourselves ought to be willing to take a close, new look at the situation if only to test the logical strength of your current positions."

The boy mumbled a couple of other questions, and Muste invited the other marble-rollers to ask a few. The questions became noticeably less aggressive. After the formal program had ended, the leader of the claque and several of his lieutenants came to Muste and apologized. For two more hours, sixty students remained to discuss additional points with Muste. Among them were a number from the considerably chastened R.O.T.C. delegation.

19

LABORATORIES
OF NONVIOLENCE

"My Dear Friends, Do Not Believe Absolutely This Dirty Official and His Common Demagogic Phrases. Go Your Path. We Are with You."

KENNETH KAUNDA, head of the United National Independence Party of Northern Rhodesia, is one of the few African nationalists who is thoroughly committed to nonviolence in all areas of his activity, personal and political. During a visit to appear before the United Nations in 1961, Kaunda made time in his tight schedule for a long session with A. J. Muste. They had previously discussed strategy for independence during a Muste visit to Africa, and Kaunda wanted to apprise Muste of the most recent developments in Northern Rhodesia.

After the meeting, Kaunda, though weary, had more appointments to keep. He was stopped by a member of the War Resisters League—a young man who had been drawn into the peace movement primarily through hearing and reading Muste. The new recruit asked

Kaunda if he did not ever despair of nonviolence as an ultimately effective technique for either his country's independence or the international abolition of war.

"There are, of course, many disappointments," Kaunda answered. "I take the view, however, that the nonviolent movement is a big experiment. And just as we would in any other experiment of this scope and difficulty, we're bound to fail sometimes. Many times. When we fail, we must find out why, and improve our methods—just as is done in any laboratory. If you believe, as I do, that violence and the threat of violence cannot solve any of our basic problems, you have no choice but to go on experimenting all the time."

Muste agreed emphatically because Kaunda had expressed Muste's own convictions on the need for continued experimentation and the avoidance of mechanical patterns of action in utilizing "negative power." Accordingly, in the past three years, the projects with which Muste has been most closely involved have been increasingly bold and hazardous. There was, for example, the unprecedentedly ambitious San Francisco to Moscow Peace Walk. The idea had germinated during the Polaris Action demonstrations in New England during the summer of 1960. The Walk itself began in San Francisco on December 1, 1960. By the time the Walkers left Moscow on October 8, 1961, the journey had taken 6,000 miles and had involved the crossing of six national frontiers.

From the beginning, Muste was an active participant in the planning and financing of the Walk which was essentially a project of the Committee for Nonviolent Action. There were several reasons why Muste thought the experiment vital. "We have been asked so often," he pointed out while the project was still being organized, "why we do not bring our message to Russia.

My answer has been, 'We are telling it to you, and what are *you* going to do about it?' But we *are* also telling it to the Soviet Union. We have tried before, and with this Walk, we try again."

Secondly, Muste and other members of C.N.V.A. regarded the Walk as a particularly dramatic way of communicating their ideas to more people in America and abroad than any previous direct-action experiment had been able to. "The symbolism of this Walk," Muste predicted, "will break through to many people who haven't been thinking in terms of nuclear pacifism. It's effective because it moves. People are *out* there walking. I expect to do a few miles myself as they get to New York. Of course," he barely suppressed a grin, "we don't expect to walk across the water at that point."

Another important element of the Walk, Muste emphasized, was to be "its function as an experiment in international action by pacifist groups which, for the most part, have so far operated only within their respective national borders."

It took the team six months to reach New York. Originally there were ten participants, but the number grew—and continued fluctuating—as the Walkers traveled. Local reaction varied during the arduous trip, but some people were clearly reached. One, John Beecher, a poet and a lecturer in English at Arizona State University, resigned his post to join the Walk with his wife. "I deeply regret the necessity of leaving my students in the middle of the academic year," he explained. "I believe, however, that my example in joining the Peace Walk will be more effective teaching than anything I might accomplish in the classroom."

Milton Mayer reported in *Liberation* on the effect of the Walk in small towns on the Monterey Peninsula. His description applied to many more communities en route.

"What was spectacular," Mayer wrote, "on each of the main streets we marched was the show of very deep sympathy by a few almost furtive individuals who, up until then, had been living respectable lives: a druggist who came out of his store and handed each Walker a calendar, a jeweler who came out of his shop and handed each Walker a batch of matches. Of such occasions, and of such opportunities, is the peace movement of five or ten years from now strengthened a little." In California and elsewhere in the country, particular interest in the Walk was shown by high school and college students, and some faculty members as well. As Mayer says, there is no doubt that the Walk served as a breeder of doubts and perhaps of a sizable number of pacifists to come.

As soon as the team arrived in New York—after having picketed the Pentagon two weeks before—fifteen Walkers were flown to Europe. Arriving in London on June 1, the Americans were joined on their European route by demonstrators from Britain, France, Belgium, Holland, Norway, West Germany, Sweden, and Finland. Not all stayed the entire distance, but there were thirty Walkers when, on September 15, the team crossed from the Polish town of Terespol into the Soviet Union. "It marked," the *War Resisters League News* observed, "the first time that placards and leaflets urging Russia to disarm unilaterally appeared in the Soviet Union."

Muste had been what European correspondent Joseph Barry called "the advance pillar of fire and smoke" for the Walkers. During much of the summer of 1961, Muste negotiated with government officials in Western Europe, Poland, and Russia for permission for the Walkers to cross their countries. He and other preparers of the way also checked with various *ad hoc* committees for the Walk which were set up in most of the European countries involved.

France refused entry. There was also difficulty in
East Germany. Having neared Berlin on August 13 at
the start of the Berlin crisis and refusing to bypass the
city, the Walkers were carried aboard a bus by East
German police and "deported" to a village near the
West German border. Learning that they were not to
be allowed in West Berlin either, the Walkers agreed
to arrangements made by Muste and two of their number with the East German government and boarded a
special bus to the Polish border where the Walk resumed on August 22. There had been other incidents
before reaching Russia, including some arrests in West
Germany when the Walkers defied the ban on demonstrating at military bases.

Once inside the Soviet Union, the Walkers carried
their banners and distributed some 80,000 leaflets on the
660-mile route to Moscow. Nearly every night the
demonstrators spoke to meetings ranging from 200 to
650 people, and several spontaneous street meetings
were held daily. There were even two demonstrations
against Soviet military preparations—one at a radar base
outside Moscow and the other a two-hour picket line of
silent protest in Red Square and at the Lenin mauso-
leum.

On October 5, the team participated in a 2½-hour
meeting at Moscow University. Professors and officials
of the Soviet Peace Committee kept trying to conclude
the discussion after an hour, but Soviet students
pounded their desks and insisted the meeting go on
whenever such an attempt was made. In the course of
the debate between the Walkers and Russian spokes-
men, no Soviet student stood up and disagreed with
official Soviet policy. But as one professor was asserting
that only the West was to blame for international tensions, a student quickly passed a note to one of the

Walkers. It read: "My dear friends, do not believe absolutely this dirty official and his common demagogic phrases. Go your path. We are with you."

Aside from the international publicity the San Francisco to Moscow Peace Walk achieved, even some non-pacifists agreed with the *Manchester Guardian* about the effect of the Walkers' presence in Moscow: "This is far from a trivial happening. In a dictatorship any public outbreak of forbidden ideas is significant; it becomes widely known even if nothing is reported in the press. The ideas may not make any converts; the students who are reported as saying, 'We don't agree with them, but let them talk,' probably meant what they said. What matters is that they have heard it suggested that their Government is as much at fault as those of the West."

The *New York Herald Tribune* added: "It is a long time since any group of foreigners has been permitted to challenge that enforced conformity. . . . Some of the inhabitants of Moscow have had their first taste of the kind of diversity that exists in the West. . . . Some may have heard in the pleas of the Marchers echoes of Tolstoi, of Prince Kropotkin, of Pasternak—of that Russian tradition of mystical humanitarianism. . . . In a word, through this tiny chink in the Iron Curtain, a few seminal ideas may have penetrated. They will not affect the current crisis, but they may grow."

Muste himself felt the Walk was an important, provocative experiment because it made dramatically clear to millions of people that these were people who refused to recognize national barriers. The Walkers' point, he emphasized, was: "We happen to be Americans—or English, French, and so on—but first of all and essentially we are human beings. We feel free to go anywhere on the face of the planet to talk to fellow human beings." When stopped, as in France, they tried to enter anyway in an unsuccessful but diligent attempt to commit civil disobedience by swimming to shore. That demonstration won them the title of "Swimmers for Peace" from two thousand Frenchmen watching at Le Havre.

The Walkers, moveover, having already accumulated a record of protesting American military preparations, underlined in all their European stops that they condemned *all* preparations for war—American, Russian, British, French, Chinese. The same basic pamphlet in six languages was distributed everywhere the Walkers went. Its essence, as Muste summarized it, was: "We reject any double standard of morality in relation to war preparation."

Finally, said Muste, there was no indication by the Walkers that they underestimated the reality of the Communist record and present policies. "We are," Muste wrote in *Liberation,* "realists who have always insisted that achieving disarmament and peace is not simple but a hard, revolutionary task. We are at variance at many crucial points with aspects of Communist regimes and policies of Communist states. There was no diluting or obscuring of such views, and the conclusive proof is that at numerous meetings in the Soviet Union, as in that notable one with students at Moscow University, there was intense controversy. Everybody understood that Soviet policies and Communist concepts were being challenged. Sometimes Russians in the audience, outraged at any questioning of Soviet 'peace' policy shouted 'Fascist' and 'warmonger' at Team speakers."

According to Muste, the root of the project, and all similar actions for peace, is that "the members of the team and those who backed them saw themselves in relation to all the individuals they met, saw the peoples and the nations of the earth *not under the pattern of conflict but of entrapment.* The Team members were human beings, freed of exclusive and arbitrary allegiances, who bore no sword against other human beings, who could therefore approach them with love and respect, but could also speak frankly to them. They saw the peoples, governments, nations, trapped in nationalism, in the long tradition of war, in entrenched vested interests, in mutual fear, in a runaway military technology which acted according to its own impersonal and completely amoral logic. They could say to *everybody:* Let us *unite* to save each other from this trap, to live as free men in a brotherly society on earth."

The Walk, however, was only a onetime project. For the future, Muste asked: "What are the peace forces of the United States and the West generally going to do with this lesson? What response, for example, will come from the churches, which should long ago have had their young people clamoring at the doors of Communist countries with the gospel of peace and not with H-bombs? Finally, what about an invitation to the peace councils of Communist countries to send some peace marchers over here on a perfectly frank basis that they be given an opportunity to express their views, provided they are prepared to face the same kind of challenging and questioning that our peace marchers faced over there?"

There was also a corollary insistence by Karl Meyer, one of the Walkers, that more expeditions to the Soviet Union by American peace demonstrators must be undertaken. Not only to speak to the Russians, but to spend long periods of time there. At Community Church in New York, Meyer spoke to an auditorium crowded with people welcoming the Walkers back to the United States.

Meyer refused to credit this preliminary Walk with

too much importance: "I have told you that we haven't touched the Soviet Union yet. And how could we hope to touch them when we haven't touched ourselves yet? How could we hope to reach them with our message when we haven't even reached our own souls through the fat layers of our American existence? If we want to reach them, we have to go and reach them. If we want to speak with them, we have to go and speak with them. And if we want to live in peace with them, we have to go and live in peace with them, personally disarmed, in labor and in poverty, again and again and again!"

The San Francisco to Moscow Peace Walk, in any case, intensified Muste's conviction that some kind of permanent international peace unit had to be established. An experiment in this direction was the formation at the end of 1961 of the World Peace Brigade for Nonviolent Action. From December 28 to January 2, fifty-five delegates from thirteen countries (all Western or nonaligned) met at Rumanna Friends School near Beirut, Lebanon. Among the sponsors who, for various reasons, could not attend were Bertrand Russell, Martin Buber, Danilo Dolci, and Vinoba Bhave. It was Bhave who had become the spiritual leader of India's nonviolent movement after the death of Gandhi.

Vinoba Bhave had been one of the originators of the idea of a nonviolent world force, along with Bertrand Russell, Michael Scott, and Jayaprakash Narayan, an associate of Bhave. The concept was endorsed at the triennial conference of the War Resisters International in India in 1960. At the Beirut organization meeting the next year, A. J. Muste was present as a member of the American delegation. By the end of the conference, Muste had been elected as one of the three co-chairmen of a World Council directing the International Peace Brigade. The other two were Scott and Narayan.

The Beirut meeting called for the establishment of an initial roster of a thousand volunteers prepared, Muste explained, "to give substantial blocs of time and to be on call for emergency service in international projects related to the abolition of war and the use of nonviolent attitudes and methods in the achievements of national independence and basic social change eliminating poverty and exploitation."

The theme of "entrapment" was emphasized in the Statement of Principles and Aims adopted at Beirut: "Individuals, governments, peoples are imprisoned in the habits, ideologies and institutions of violence which they themselves have devised and built. Common sense, political wisdom and profound moral imperatives compel us to break out of this condition. Men must find and be ready to experiment with an alternative. That alternative is nonviolence."

Regional offices were set up in India, London, and New York. Through them, the Brigade's organizing, proselytizing and research activities were to be channeled. By March, 1962, the nature of the Brigade's functions was further clarified: "Although it was decided that conciliatory efforts and constructive service would be a definite part of the Brigade's activities, its distinguishing characteristic would be active participation and demonstration as a nonviolent, non-national volunteer force committed in many cases to a particular 'side' or 'cause' judged most consistent with the Brigade's aims. The Brigade will remain, however, uncommitted to any political or national group in general, as well as to any laws, customs or disciplines inconsistent with the Brigade's aims, using civil disobedience as a major positive 'weapon' or method of action where judged necessary. The Brigade is not, therefore, a 'neutral' force so much as one concerned with achieving just ends through peaceful rather than violent and destructive action."

It is true that the Brigade is committed to no one set of political-economic doctrines, but there were indications at the initial Beirut conference of the general orientation of many of its supporters. Reporting in the *Jerusalem Post* from Beirut, Ann Morrisett, an experienced chronicler of the international peace movement, observed: "Though political and economic ideologies were not specifically discussed, it is no accident that mention was often made of 'cooperative commonwealth,' 'self-determination,' and 'economic and social justice.' Nor is it accidental that some of the delegates were socialists of a decentralist, anti-totalitarian nature."

The delegates to Beirut were all too aware that the Brigade was very much an experiment and that its existence could make sense only if its ideas were translated into various forms of action. In *Peace News,* Michael Randle ended a description of this first conference of the Brigade: "On New Year's night there was an attempted *coup d'état* in Beirut. Some people heard machine-gun fire in the distance. On the way down to Beirut on Tuesday morning [the day after the conference ended] there were tanks on the high ground above the city and checkpoints at four or five places. 'We're going to make your job unnecessary,' someone from the back of the coach called to the soldier who stopped the bus. He was not much more than a boy with a very young, finely featured face, and a deep olive complexion. I don't think he heard, but anyway he grinned and waved us on."

One project initiated by the World Peace Brigade early in 1962 was the establishment in Dar es Salaam, Tanganyika, of a training center for nonviolent action in the various African campaigns for independence. The center was in unique contrast to other training encampments in the Congo and elsewhere in Africa where na-

tionalists instruct recruits in multiple uses of violence—
from commando tactics through sabotage and assassina-
tion. The World Peace Brigade center was made possible
through the encouragement of Kenneth Kaunda of
Northern Rhodesia and Julius Nyerere, President of the
Tanganyika African National Union. Nyerere later became a sponsor of the World Peace Brigade. Both are
advocates of nonviolence and had been impressed at the
news of the founding of the Brigade.

The Brigade's international staff taught the techniques and philosophy of nonviolence to representatives
of several African national groups at Dar es Salaam,
and helped focus world attention on the turbulent situation in Northern Rhodesia in particular by submitting
evidence to the United Nations Committee on Colonial-
ism. There was also a plan by which the staff and their
students would engage in a nonviolent march into
Northern Rhodesia to coincide with a general strike for
independence to be called by Kaunda.

As it happened, Kaunda decided to continue negotiat-
ing with the British government, and the march did not
take place. Nonetheless, Muste declared toward the end
of 1962, "At least we gave evidence that for the first
time, non-Africans were willing to come to the support
of an African independence struggle." The presence
of the training center, moreover, gave Kaunda moral
support in his continuing difficulties with other nationalists in Northern Rhodesia who were not at all convinced of the effectiveness of a nonviolent strategy for
independence. By 1963, Kaunda was still head of his
party; and while the nationalists were not yet in full
control of Northern Rhodesia, they made considerable
headway and Kaunda was Minister of Local Government.

The World Peace Brigade's center in Dar es Salaam

has remained active, and other World Peace Brigade
projects are scheduled for the coming decade. As small
as its beginning has been, the concept of the World
Peace Brigade further proves, Muste feels, "that the essentially individualistic moral or religious pacifism,
characteristically expressing itself in conscientious objection to war, is no longer a sufficient basis for the
movement. (It has been too little realized that this type
of pacifism has been a phenomenon largely confined to
the Anglo-Saxon world and to a limited period in history.)"

Instead, Muste goes on, there now must be a nonviolent revolutionary movement which is global in composition and scope. "Of course," he recognizes, "there
must be strong movements within each country, but
a series of isolated or tenuously related national organizations and movements simply cannot deal intelligently
and seriously with the threat of war and the task of
building a sane society. There must be international
thinking, planning, action. From another angle, every
important action within a nation can now be politically
and morally strengthened by the inclusion of World
Peace Brigade volunteers. . . . None of our organizations has hitherto had a structure for concentrated and
continuous international planning and action."

The presence of Indian members on the World Peace
Brigade's Council and at the training center in Tanganyika was particularly heartening to Muste. "It is tre-
mendously important," he pointed out, "that it is also
the Gandhian movement in India which has now been
brought into living relationship with the movement in
the United States and the United Kingdom, because
this immediately gives us a base in Asia and a relationship to Africa of a kind which Western peace movements did not and could not have. Therefore it makes it

global in a sense which it would not otherwise be, both actually and potentially. . . . A beginning has been made in realizing Gandhi's concept of a world *Shanti sena* (peace army)."

In the summer of 1962, the World Peace Brigade— along with leading Indian Gandhians, the Committee for Nonviolent Action, the War Resisters International, the British Campaign for Nuclear Disarmament, and the British Committee of 100—became one of the sponsors of the voyage of *Everyman III*. The ship, captained by anthropologist Earle Reynolds, left London the following September 26 with an international crew. It was headed for Leningrad to protest Soviet nuclear testing. The voyage was a continuation of those seaborne experiments in direct action in 1958 which had included the demonstrations against American nuclear tests by the *Golden Rule* and the *Phoenix* (the latter directed by the same Earle Reynolds).

Everyman III, in fact, followed two abortive attempts earlier in 1962 to demonstrate against American tests by *Everyman I* and *Everyman II*. These two odysseys had been largely organized by the Committee for Non- violent Action, and A. J. Muste had once again aided in the strategy and fund-raising for the projects.

In one of the letters he sent out in the spring of 1962, Muste observed: "This is a good time to be reminded of the amazing statement which *Life* magazine made on August 20, 1945. Under the first shock of the bombs that fell on Hiroshima and Nagasaki, it declared that our *'sole safeguard* against the very real danger of a reversion to barbarism is the kind of morality which compels the individual conscience, be the group right or wrong.' The writer looked for a moment at this pre- posterous sentence he had written for *Life* and asked himself and the rest of us: 'The individual conscience against the atomic bomb?' Then he reaffirmed it: 'Yes, there is no other way.' If 'the group,' the nation, was wrong in that summer of 1945, it is much more wrong in this spring of 1962 in exploding bombs and launching missiles in comparison with which the instruments of 1945 were firecrackers and crates. . . . We *must* get that ship into the Pacific. Others should be built or bought and ready in case the authorities conclude this one must be stopped."

The authorities did so conclude and enforced their convictions by means which were quite debatable legally (for a full account, see W. S. Merwin's, "Act of Conscience: The Story of Everyman," in the December 29, 1962, *Nation*). The plywood, thirty-foot sailing boat, built by C.N.V.A. supporters, never got near Christmas Island, its destination. The first crew of three was stopped about fifteen miles off the California coast on May 26, and served thirty-day jail terms. A second crew defied a court order shortly after midnight on July 4, but a combination of seasickness, faulty equipment and lack of navigational experience forced them to turn back the next day from a point 150 miles off California. The members of that crew received sixty-day jail terms.

Undaunted by the initial failure of *Everyman I*, the Committee for Nonviolent Action sent out *Everyman II* from Honolulu on June 23. This 28-foot ketch did enter the Johnston Island testing area three days later, but was seized by the Coast Guard on June 29. Its crew was fined, and jailed for refusal to pay the fine. After spending five to eighteen days in jail, the three men were released pending appeal.

It was with this background of frustration that *Everyman III* with Earle Reynolds was prepared. This ship did reach its destination—Leningrad—on October 19. But the twelve men on board were denied visas by the

Russians. Refusing to cooperate in their expulsion, they tried to scuttle their ship as it was being towed out of the harbor. Russian officials prevented the ship from sinking, imprisoned the crew on board for eight days, and finally towed the ship into international waters where its crew reluctantly resumed command and sailed to Stockholm.

On the face of it, the record of the three *Everyman* voyages appears dismal. Yet Muste and his colleagues felt that the dramatic nature of this kind of protest had brought the movement more public attention. "Our basic policy," Muste reaffirmed, "is to bear witness in every land and to appeal to the conscience of our fellow human beings everywhere."

Yet, even to many who are sympathetic to the various peace groups involved, such demonstrations seem to be of minute use. There is evidence, on the other hand, that some individuals have been changed by their example. Radio engineer Evan Yoes, Jr., of the crew of *Everyman I* had, for example, been drawn to volunteer because he had remembered the Nevada Protest which A. J. Muste had helped organize on the 1957 anniversary of the bombing of Hiroshima. At the time, Yoes had considered the protest absurd; but through the years, it began to make more sense to him until he finally offered himself to C.N.V.A. for assignment on *Everyman I*.

To those who would point out that personal conversions such as that of Mr. Yoes are exceedingly few, Muste would answer that the movement can only sustain itself and grow by affecting a profound change in individuals. Accordingly, each new "reconstructed" person cannot but be an index, however slight, of progress. Muste adds that there is no telling how many people actually are influenced by this quality of personal witnessing. The nucleus of revolutionary thought may thereby be planted in thousands who may yet be ready —if there is time—for the "new society."

Seemingly impregnable, however, is the vast majority of *this* society—those who either agree with the concept of deterrence or feel entirely impotent to change the course of their government's policy. There are also those for whom a San Franciscan, interviewed by W. S. Merwin for his report on *Everyman I,* serves as spokesman. Referring to the peace agitators, the man said: "I guess they're the conscience of the country. On the other hand a conscience is a liability. You can't run a business with a conscience. I've compromised with mine all my life. We see things that are wrong, but we don't do anything about it. A conscience is a thing to brag about at banquets, but it's too uncomfortable to live with, for most of us. Those people down there, they're trying to wake up our consciences, but it won't work because what most of us want is to deaden them. Maybe that's why the human race isn't justified in looking forward to a long and happy future. They've temporized with everything. It's too late for an act of conscience, any act of conscience, to be effective any longer."

20

THE NEW
SOCIETY

*"We Are Not Engaged in Seeking Power,
in Taking Over the Institutions and the
Instruments of Power, Not Even in Order
to Use Them for Our Own Supposedly
Noble Ends."*

MUSTE's years as a Trotskyite left in him a deep and
enduring distrust that "the new society" could be
achieved by any all-encompassing socioeconomic-politi-
cal blueprint. He is convinced, in the first place, that
the vintage Marxist concept of class conflict as a basic
stimulus to pervasively radical alteration of the social
structure—and the people in it—has not been proved in
the West. Furthermore, as other areas of the world become industrialized, there is no indication that class
conflict alone will bring about the millenium outside
the West either.

In America, for example, "in the economic sphere,"
Muste has written in *Liberation*, "there are multitudes
who have, on the one hand, a considerable vested interest and who, on the other, are in hock to the system

and do not feel free to revolt. The unions are themselves integrally tied in with the economic system, including its defense aspects, and are in no sense instruments for revolt. To some extent the trade-union movement actually stands in the way of organizing the unorganized, and I do not see any reason to think that if office and service workers, farm labor, and Negroes were to be organized, they would constitute an instrument for revolt. Most Negroes, we may observe in passing, want to become a part of the American affluent society, not to revolutionize it."

So far as Muste's central preoccupation, war, is concerned, he points out that "whether you look at the countries where there are strong Labor or Socialist parties, or whether you look at the Communist countries, the expectation that advance in the direction of Socialism of one form or another would lead to the elimination of war has not been realized. Generally speaking, the Socialist and Labor parties have tended to identify themselves with the state, especially with the state's foreign policy, and have not radically opposed their military establishments."

It is not that Muste has lost his conviction that social change will have to involve economic and other forms of planning. "Disarmament," he underlines, "cannot be achieved nor can the problem of war be resolved without being accompanied by profound changes in the economic order and in the structure of society. . . . In the United States, for example, it is obvious that much more planning will have to be accepted if there is to be a transformation from a war to a peace economy." Similarly, in the Soviet Union, "the internal structure of society could not possibly remain what it is if the Soviet military establishment was removed."

What Muste *is* saying, and has been for the past decade, is that such classic spurs to revolution as the working class or Socialist political parties can no longer be counted on to direct the way. The source of the new momentum, Muste preaches, will be the peace movement. "There is now no Socialist and Labor movement committed to basic social change, and therefore the peace movement either has to take part in the development of new political forces and new political organizations, or it has itself to be somehow or other a force for political change in the sense in which the peace movement was not in the old days—when pacifism was an individual matter."

Muste may be correct, at least in part. For all the attempts to strengthen and revivify "the Left" in the West, most of the enthusiastic young who are radical (however inchoate their ideology) are more attracted to the various peace and nonviolent groups than to any political party. This is especially true in America and Great Britain, and there are signs of similar, nascent activity among the young in other European countries. These are the young who would agree with Muste that "We cannot have peace if we are only concerned with peace. War is not an accident. It is the logical outcome of a certain way of life. If we want to attack war, we have to attack that way of life."

The difficulty is that Muste remains vague as to how this rising reservoir of desire for social dislocation is going to be channeled into any meaningful, positive action.

"We are not engaged," Muste has written, "in seeking power, in taking over the institutions and the instruments of power, not even in order to use them for **our own** supposedly noble ends. We are truly committed to organizing life on the basis of love and not power. . . . It is a new kind of society, not a change of government that we seek."

Muste is realistic enough to recognize that in any basically effective sense—so far as social dislocation is concerned—"there is no peace movement in the world today which influences day-to-day government policy definitely away from the Cold War. We do not have a movement. A movement has to be built. It can only be built on a clear facing of where we are and what needs to be done, on an understanding that a revolutionary task is before us and a task of massive conversion, of changing the focus of man's thinking and aspirations."

While a study of Muste's writings and speeches provides "a clear facing of where we are," it has few directions about "what needs to be done." He does say: "It is quite true that we can only dimly discern what the new society will be like. This has always been true in revolutionary periods. The future did not correspond to the blueprints if men ventured to make blueprints. This is as it should be because like Abraham and other men of faith, we do not want to stay in or go back to the City—which is all we are, alas, familiar with and which is doomed. This is the one temptation we must not succumb to. It is better to go out, not knowing whither we go, precisely because the city of peace and fraternity which we seek has yet to be built and must not be like what we now know and can readily describe."

On another occasion, Muste emphasized: "You have to take each situation as it comes. I do not have a 'master plan' for the revolution I work for, but I say again that the concept of men manufacturing a social order which they have planned and decided to realize is repugnant to the nonviolent or Gandhian concept of history and sociopolitical development."

Muste has elaborated on this argument in *Liberation:* "As Joan V. Bondurant pointed out in her *Conquest of Violence,* nonviolence does not postulate an end, which is formulated as an 'ism,' or conceived as the ideal goal and therefore to be attained by whatever means are deemed necessary. Nonviolence is a means for dealing with actual situations, with tension and conflict, which indeed influences the character of the outcome, but the 'end' remains 'open-ended,' so to speak. It does not harden and become absolutized into an 'ism' to which human beings have to be subjected. Looked at from another angle, this means the constant effort to involve human beings themselves, the 'people,' in the decision process, and to subject them to the discipline which such meaningful participation implies rather than to external and institutional pressures."

As one example of the kind of open-ended activity which he approves, Muste has observed that "when India approached the day of independence, Gandhi proposed to the Congress Party, which had been the organizational instrument of the struggle for freedom, that it should not take power, form a government along essentially conventional lines and function as a political party in office—and naturally wanting to stay in office. He proposed that it become an organization of 'Servants' who would work at the social base to heal communal strife, develop 'basic education' suited to the Indian people and their condition, remove caste distinctions, build economic equality and village democracy. . . . This was a very revolutionary proposal. It seems to me that far too little attention has been paid to it in India and outside as well. The Congress Party leadership, headed by such men as Nehru and Patel, did not accept Gandhi's proposal. In a sense all that has followed in Indian political life stems from that decision."

At base, whatever open-end projects he may support at particular times and places, Muste's views are consonant with a statement by Jayaprakash Narayan: "No government can be expected to embrace nonviolence. If nonviolent action has to be taken, the people alone can take it."

It is one thing, however, to be suspicious of blueprints and institutionalized power, but it is quite something else to call for action and then to present only a hazy vision of the future. So far, in fact, the bulk of Muste's strategy has involved protest against present power with few constructive ideas on how to achieve—let alone how to recognize—the "profound changes in the economic order and in the structure of society to come."

Muste has, for instance, urged young men in large numbers to give notice "that they *refuse* to be drafted, refuse to register or carry draft cards, and for young women publicly to join them when they do so." Similarly, Muste has called for "workers to quit war jobs and for scientists and technicians to be more scrupulous about the kind of research or technical work they do. This is a time for the Society for Social Responsibility in Science to call for thousands of new members. Now is the time for many more people to practice tax refusal in one or another form." And always, he summons people "to get on the streets and demonstrate."

These adjurations, however, have all been for the exercise of "negative power." And while it is true that some positive activities may be in prospect for the World Peace Brigade in terms of assisting specific projects in social reconstruction, the Brigade is still very limited in resources.

There has, in sum, been far too little in Muste's theoretical work in recent years to provide an answer to Paul Goodman's serious charge that "the peace movement is at present astoundingly negative: 'strike for peace' means merely 'refuse the Cold War.' The most popular slogan is Ban the Bomb, and there is a rising realization that Peace Must Come from the People. But the idea of positively waging peace—in acts of community-forming, new culture, political reconstruction, economic conversion—seems not yet to take hold of the popular feeling.

"Yet," Goodman continues, "it is psychologically and sociologically evident that the war spirit is energized by profound frustrations and anxieties of moral and civil life; that the extraordinary apathy of the vast majority to their danger is a result of institutions that have fragmented community and made people feel powerless; and that the only economy possible, under the present control, is the Cold War economy. Really to relax the Cold War requires withdrawing energy from its causes. Hard thinkers in fact propose real satisfactions, more practical institutions, a productive use of technology, and so forth. Yet these ideas are not importantly part of the peace movement."

Nor has any leader of the peace movement, Muste included, effectively rebutted Norman Thomas' assertion: "It's by politics that we'll have peace or war in the end, no matter how much good will is diffused." Yet, as Paul Goodman notes, "although the peace movement cuts across class-lines, color-lines, and national-lines, and is non-conformist and raggedly organized, I do not as yet see that it presages any particular political shape."

In his charge to the peace movement, Goodman did make an essential point, an analysis which leads to an understanding of Muste's own most vital function. "Apparently," Goodman wrote, "it is first necessary, at least in America, for hundreds of thousands of people to break loose, by merely negative action, from the mesmerism of affluent powerlessness. . . . This impotence *is* the Cold War."

Muste is very much aware of the growing dissatisfaction among peace workers, especially the younger recruits, with the lack of concrete plans for changing the society. "I agree," he says, "that while avoiding a blueprint, we do have to try to be more specific about the kind of society which we are trying to build. In my own case, I come to a position which is closer to a social democratic perspective than an anarchist one. My view, however, would involve a very considerable decentralization of power. But I admit that we need *new* ideas and we need to make better use of the kind of material concerning the 'new society' which we can find in such writers as Lewis Mumford and Paul Goodman.

"The core of our problem," Muste adds, "is that if we say we are not just seeking to take over the existing instruments of power in order to use them for presumably better ends, how *can* we effect a transition to a different kind of society? We have to remember that we cannot accomplish this change by inaugurating a campaign, so to speak. We cannot by ourselves *create* a situation in which a particular society or part of a society will actually set itself to dealing with the problem of organizing human life in a new way. We cannot manufacture these conditions, either by having the future all figured out on paper or by trying to devise clever, effective ways to bring society to the point of making a change."

Muste is convinced that "it will be factors in the objective situation which will ultimately make it possible for enough people to wake up to the fact that the road they're on leads to a dead end and must be abandoned.

There is no doubt in my mind that we are in a pre-revolutionary situation right now. The game is played out, just as it was for the Czar on the eve of the Russian revolution. I don't mean that fundamental social change will begin to happen just because many people finally recognize in the abstract the full horrors of nuclear war. To expect change on that basis would be depending on magic. I do feel, however, that objective events—perhaps a terrible nuclear accident—may open the eyes of a sizable enough number of people before it's too late.

"The peace movement," Muste goes on, "must be ready with more than slogans when the objective situation does begin to galvanize the society toward revolution. And the peace movement will have to operate on the basis of a realistic analysis of what needs to be done. There is no easy, cheap price for peace. A society in which there is no war will involve very radical changes all around, and hard thinking has to be done now, not only by pacifists, but by such specialists as economists and psychologists. It is the kind of planning that will involve such specialized United Nations agencies as the World Health Organization, the Food and Agriculture Organization, UNICEF, and the Technical Assistance program.

"If we indeed do have the time," Muste feels, "there will have to be a new society. There are already indications of thaw in many different areas. In the field of mental illness, for one example, there has been a movement completely away from the old ideas of how to treat those who are seriously disturbed to the point of psychosis. Current techniques in that specialty constitute what is in effect a nonviolent approach. This is what happens in a prerevolutionary period. Many changes occur in many different areas which appear to

be unrelated; but when the time comes, they all fit together into a pattern because the objective situation has
reached that point when the revolution itself begins."

For all of his cognizance of the need for more concrete planning by the peace movement, Muste grants
that his own work has largely been—and remains—focused on preparing a climate for change rather than in
exploring the specifics of that change. Insofar as the
"new society" is concerned, the cumulative value of
Muste's efforts has been based on his ability—primarily
by force of personal example and its effects on others
who themselves become proselytizers—to stimulate more
and more Americans "to break loose." Even if this resistance to "the mesmerism of affluent powerlessness" is
so far being reflected almost entirely in negative action,
it has at least helped to create a nucleus of those who are
ready for profound social change.

In essence, Muste has enabled more and more Americans to regain a sense of their own power to make a
decision in a world in which the most fundamental decisions are now in the hands of only a very few. So far,
this resurgence of the idea of the individual as decision-
maker has been almost entirely by way of protest. But
at least the assertion of the right to refuse approval is
a degree above the acceptance of total personal impotence in the area of war and peace.

In his acceptance speech of the War Resisters League
1958 Peace Award, Muste quoted approvingly the credo
of the late C. Wright Mills. Mills had called on everyone, especially intellectuals and scientists, to become
conscientious objectors to the concept and practice of
nuclear deterrence. "If you do not do it," Mills had
said, "you at least are not responsible for its being done.
If you refuse to do so out loud, others may refrain
quietly from doing it, and those who still do it may

then do it only with hesitation and guilt. . . . To refuse to do it is an act affirming yourself as a moral center of responsible decisions . . . it is the act of a man who rejects 'fate,' for it reveals the resolution of one human being to take at least his own fate into his own hands."

On another occasion, Muste put the terms of this essential decision into his own words: "Precisely in a day when the individual appears to be utterly helpless, to 'have no choice,' when the aim of the 'system' is to convince him that he is helpless as an individual and that the only way to meet regimentation is by regimentation, there is absolutely no hope save in going back to the beginning. The human being, the child of God, must assert his humanity and his sonship again. He must exercise the choice which he no longer has as something accorded him by society, which he 'naked, weaponless, armourless, without shield or spear, but only with naked hands and open eyes' must create again. He must understand that this naked human being is the one *real* thing in the face of the mechanics and the mechanized institutions of our age."

Once having made that decision, more and more young recruits to the peace movement are searching eagerly and anxiously for collective ways so to alter the society that war will be impossible. They want to do more than demonstrate. Muste, however, has drawn for them no detailed routes into the future. He is able to say of himself what Eugene Debs once said: "I would not be a Moses to lead you into the Promised Land, because if I could lead you into it, someone else could lead you out of it."

Whatever the composition of "the new city"—if any —there is still an enormous amount of work to be done here and now in finding more recruits for the journey. Muste—and through him, his colleagues and disciples

—continues to teach more and more of the young to be responsible for their own ideas and actions. It is surely a vital function, and it may well be unjust to expect more of any one man in his lifetime.

21

ENDING THE EIGHTH DECADE

"We Are Living on the Edge of the Abyss All the Time, Though It Is Only Occasionally That the Sky Is Lit Up So That We Can See It."

ALTHOUGH his reserve of stamina occasionally seems somewhat depleted, it is difficult to realize that A. J. Muste will soon be an octogenarian. In the summer of 1962, his doctor, as a colleague of Muste put it, "told A.J. to put on the brakes. But A.J. put his foot on the accelerator instead." There is, in sum, no diminution in Muste's enthusiam for his peripatetic role as an international agitator for peace. Despite more evident and more frequent signs of weariness, Muste continues his unceasing rounds of committee meetings and trips along with his flow of articles and correspondence.

A teen-ager, newly recruited to the nuclear pacifists, watched Muste address a demonstration across the street from the United Nations in the spring of 1962. The meeting was in protest against both Russian and American testing. A portable microphone brought by the peacemakers was not working. "It's a drag," the young-ster said. "A.J.'s voice won't be able to carry." Yet, when Muste began to speak, his voice—though soft—was clear and strong enough to reach nearly all of the several hundred participants in the demonstration.

Toward the end of his brief talk, Muste's voice rose in volume and intensity, and everyone could hear him assert: "It is often said that those of us who are here are weak and cowardly. I say it is we who refuse to surrender to war who are strong. It is those who do not demonstrate for peace who are soft and weak and cow-ardly."

"It's hard," the teen-ager said, applauding, "to be-lieve he's really that old." David McReynolds of the War Resisters League, some five decades younger than Muste, adds with unabated surprise: "The guy just doesn't *get* old. He was seventy-two when I first began to work with him and I kept waiting for the obvious signs of old age. I finally stopped waiting."

"A.J. is a wonder," adds A. Philip Randolph. "He picks up and goes to Africa or France like you'd go downtown." "If anything," adds Robert Gilmore, Ex-ecutive Director of Turn Toward Peace, "A.J. makes fun of his age. I once kept him waiting at an appoint-ment in Harlem. It was raining hard, and he was stand-ing, hunched over, the water dripping down his hat. 'Fine thing,' he tried to grumble, 'keeping an old man waiting.' Then he looked up and laughed. In time you forget his age. That's why nobody treats him as a 'grand old man.' He not only doesn't ask for that kind of han-dling, but he'd probably be hurt if he got it. He doesn't want deference; he just wants to be an active part of whatever is going on."

"Unlike several of the older, revered radicals," Ralph Di Gia of the War Resisters League points out, "A.J. is always accessible by phone. You don't have to go through a secretary. And he's always willing to do the smallest things—write a letter or make a phone call—if he thinks it'll help. Sometimes I think he's *too* accessible."

Younger peace workers are still particularly attracted to Muste, not only because he is always available to them, but as David McReynolds says, "because he's much more contemporary in his thinking than nearly all the other elders of the movement. You never hear him say, 'When you've been around as long as I have, you'll realize that. . . .' He doesn't give you the answers of twenty and thirty years ago." Accordingly, it is no surprise to see Muste listed on the National Advisory Council of the growing Student Peace Union (over 5,000 members). Equally predictable is the fact that Muste helps the S.P.U. raise funds.

Muste is also resolutely aware of current argot among the young. His secretary, Edith Snyder, a graduate of Brooklyn College, where she majored in philosophy, is amused when Muste says in the course of his dictation, "I don't want to keep you hung up on this," "I hope this doesn't bug you," or "we certainly had a ball."

Despite the impression Muste gives of wanting to be the Nestor of all peace activity, he does not, the younger radical pacifists feel, try to prevent the rise of new leadership. "He likes his position as the country's number one pacifist," says a young, active strategist in the Committee for Nonviolent Action, "but, at the same time, he feels no threat to his position, and he keeps encouraging new people to join and help direct the movement." An older figure in peace action admires Muste's lack of a power complex, but admits that in his own case, "seeing all these young people come in makes me nervous. I'm afraid A.J.'s more flexible than I am.

I felt more secure when there were only ten or fifteen of us involved in all the major peace actions. Now the nucleus is growing, and most of those newer leaders came in with his encouragement."

Bayard Rustin, who has been closer to Muste than any other radical pacifist in recent years, is convinced that "A.J.'s encouragement of young people is basically connected with the fact that he is so fundamentally a revolutionary. He has always been frustrated by American society, and still hopes to help start a workable political organization that will have nonviolence as one of its key elements. That's why he jumps from one thing to another. He keeps hoping this next group will be *the* one leading to a new alignment of forces. He feels that a political, economic and spiritual revolution must come because the need is so great. And that's why he's so involved with the young. Every time he meets a youngster who seems to have potentially revolutionary ideas, he cultivates him as a sort of moral obligation. To him they're all recruits for the time when the revolution can really begin."

"There's something apocalyptic, in fact, in the way he talks, even when the young aren't around," says John Oliver Nelson, of Yale. "It's as if he were John the Baptist telling us we are not the ones who are to come but that we must prepare for those who will."

As has been true all his life, Muste continues to find his recruits among the nonreligious young as well as those who believe in a God. His secretary, Edith Snyder, for example, is an atheist and flinches when Muste finishes a letter, as he sometimes does, with a reference to man's unworthiness in the sight of God. "I don't know what he means by that. There are a lot of good things in us as well as bad. I don't feel that we're that unworthy, and I don't know what he means by God. But I can't deny the fact that I love the man and that without proselytizing, he's caused a basic change in me."

Soon after she had started working for Muste, Miss Snyder was confronted by a friend of Muste, a woman who is active in several peace organizations.

"And are you a Christian?" asked the lady.

"No," said Miss Snyder.

"Are you a pacifist?"

"No."

"A world federalist?" the visitor asked hopefully.

"No."

"Well," the lady said determinedly, "A.J. will set you right."

"I guess he has," Miss Snyder admits. "At first, it was just watching him that made me realize how good a person can be without being self-righteous. Also, before I knew him, I thought all pacifists were crackpots or fanatics. Every time I had a question about pacifism or nonviolent action, he'd talk to me as long as was necessary to make his points clear. It didn't matter how busy he was. And it was always I, not he, who initiated the discussion. I still don't have the degree of faith in people that he has, but now I'm close to being a pacifist. I would not call myself that, because for me to term myself a pacifist when A.J. is one would be the height of hubris. I expect I've also been affected by A.J. in my attitude toward religion. I remain nonreligious, but knowing him has made me realize what religion can be and what it can mean to someone open to it. In A.J.'s case, religion really does become a spiritual, creative force."

Further describing the cumulative effect on her of Muste's example, Miss Snyder speaks for many younger people in the peace movement who have come to know Muste. "A few years ago," she noted at the beginning of 1963, "I began to participate in demonstrations by handing out leaflets at a civil defense protest demonstration. But then I took shelter. I guess I wondered what everybody would say if I were arrested. Gradually, I came to realize that I didn't have to make excuses to other people. What counts is what *I* think. Therefore, by 1961, I was able to refuse to take shelter. I couldn't make any more excuses for myself. At Brooklyn College, several students, myself included, were suspended for five days because we wouldn't go inside. Some five hundred kids showed up for that demonstration, and only a handful took shelter. I had helped organize it. The next morning, when I came to work, A.J. kissed me. 'You're wonderful,' he said. 'What did I do?' 'You got suspended,' he answered. Gee, you'd think I'd done something marvelous."

Miss Snyder is impressed but somewhat troubled at her employer's refusal to react in anger when provoked. "We once sent a petition to several important people," she says, "asking them to protest the beating of a Negro labor leader in the South. The president of a prominent girl's school wrote back that she deplored the incident, but couldn't give her name because the school was raising funds and she didn't want to risk offending any potential contributors. I was furious. When A.J. began dictating his answer, I said, 'Give her hell.'

"But he didn't. To be sure, his letter was an implicit reprimand, but he didn't clobber her. I'm not like that. Even little things get me angry. But nothing seems to break through his composure. Even when he's under a lot of pressure and has millions of things on his mind, he remains extraordinarily organized. The phones can be ringing and letters have to be answered, but no matter how many times he's interrupted, he never says, 'Now where was I?' The dictation keeps flowing; he always knows what he's going to say."

When Muste does allow himself time away from work and the telephone, he enjoys the theater, movies, opera (particularly Wagner), and is interested in nearly all forms of dance from Martha Graham to the Bolshoi Ballet. Occasionally he'll play anagrams with a close friend such as Cara Cook. "He plays as hard as he works," she says, "and gets rather annoyed when I beat him, which is most of the time. He once tried to get 'coffier' by me, and I told him there was no such word. 'Yes, there is,' he insisted. 'I hear it on the radio all the time.'"

Muste reads a great deal, usually in politics, international affairs, the philosophy of history, theology, and Marxism. He tries to avoid novels because, once he starts a story, he's generally impelled to finish it at one sitting. Somehow Muste does manage to read nearly all the reports, pamphlets, and other pacifist literature that arrive in the daily mail. He usually disappears at lunch, taking a pile of papers to the nearest Schrafft's. "I choose Schrafft's," Muste once told a friend, "because their portions are smaller. I can't eat a lot of heavy food, but I also hate to waste food. Schrafft's, therefore, is just right for me."

A comprehensive newspaper reader, Muste marks up the pages and clips out passages he considers significant. He puts the cutouts in a pocket file, and occasionally mimeographs one of them for his personal mailing list.

As a result of the mailing list and the ceaseless rounds of speeches and conferences, Muste appears to have friends everywhere in the country. A couple of summers ago, he was visiting Cara Cook and her family in a small Maine village, forty miles from Portland. "I hadn't expected anyone to know him there," she says, "but after church, two people suddenly shouted after us, 'A.J., A.J.!' They'd met him at a conference somewhere. I'm less surprised, however, at how many people know him than that he always remembers *their* names."

Roy Finch, an observer with Muste at the 1957 Communist Party convention, was unprepared for the number of friends Muste had on the floor. "Even though his anti-Communism had been so well known through the years, a lot of the old-time Communist radicals greeted him warmly. I guess they were the ones for whom it was too late temperamentally to get out of the party. They seemed so pleased to establish contact with A.J. again."

Although Muste has many friends in a wide variety of radical settings, he is never, as George Houser of the American Committee on Africa says, "a granddaddy with open arms to take in lost souls. Nor is he the sort of man you'd slap on the back. It's not that he's austere, but very few people get familiar with A.J. There's a detachment in most of his personal relations. Also, he's not given to small talk. It's as if he always has his mind on more cosmic affairs. He is considerate and helpful, but I can't imagine his ever putting his arm around you. Conversely, I can't imagine his ever snapping at you either."

While it's true that Muste is rarely ruffled, he has at times been caught "in the grip of righteous indignation," as one old friend describes the occasions when Muste begins lecturing an opponent, sticking a long forefinger in the offender's face. Muste is also capable of telling a stubbornly dissident peace worker, "You stand in the way." Even when Muste does show passion in debate, however, the emotions sometimes appear to be part of his plan of argument. "His is sort of a strategic excitement," says Roy Finch, who has been involved with Muste in policy disagreements. "There's passion there, but it's always controlled. It's true that he doesn't easily give ground. He learned a lot from all those years in radical politics. He wasn't then, and he isn't now, a sentimentalist in any way. Basically, he's a political personality who is convinced that the central political issue is war."

Although Muste's ideas remain radical and his techniques of persuasion can be forceful, the initial impression he gives is deceptively bland. At committee meetings, Muste is usually the last to speak, and then he often combines previous viewpoints into a workable plan. In public, he avoids the more overtly dramatic platform techniques of many experienced speechmakers, including several in the peace movement, and instead talks slowly with an inexorable logic that on some nights can be absorbingly effective.

In personal discussion, for all his disinclination to yield when he has reached a decision and the occasional tightening of his voice in moments of annoyance, Muste is usually an excellent listener before he begins to argue. "The unique thing about A.J.," says labor leader Sidney Lens, "is that you never feel you're retreating when you talk with him. He's about the only radical I know who doesn't threaten other people's egos. He doesn't overwhelm you. In fact, you can talk at him for two hours and he won't interrupt. He'll listen and listen, and, if you don't know him, you'll begin wondering if this old guy has all his marbles. But eventually, he'll make very clear what he thinks. Similarly, at a meeting, he can sit as part of the group on the platform without towering over it, and yet he winds up having been the key figure there."

"I would say," Norman Thomas concluded an assessment of Muste a couple of years ago, "that A.J.'s major achievement has been in being himself." "And the base of that self," adds Roy Finch, "is his sense of principle.

This is an awfully smooth world and contains very few men of absolute principle. A.J. has stood so far on that absolute end of the spectrum of principle that he's influenced thousands of people to at least move in his direction, and they have influenced others. Most of us never have to—or don't—take much of a moral stand in the course of our lives. Therefore, we don't build up the collective moral strength of our society. A.J. does. He builds up everybody's backbone."

Around the time of Muste's seventy-seventh birthday, several of his friends were arguing about how much he had actually accomplished in his life. "Certainly," said one, "he's not an overpowering historical figure. He's always been in minority movements, and he always would be if he lived forever."

Another disagreed: "In a different era with more discontent, A.J. would have been a Gandhi. Even though we don't have much time now, that time is not yet ripe for A.J."

A nonpacifist present, a man of Muste's age, shook his head negatively. "A.J.'s a failure in terms of realistic action because he's a romantic. The amount of human compassion he has can lead you to sup with the devil, and I don't sup with the devil."

"That's exactly it," a much younger man, a pacifist, said. "A.J. *would* sup with the devil. What's he got to be afraid of? I'll tell you what it is that A.J. has done. He's whipped life. He's never defeated. He keeps riding the wave."

Muste laughed when he heard of his critic's complaint that he might break bread with the devil. "I know what he means," Muste said. "He's never forgotten the American Forum and my meetings with the Communists. Well, I've never thought one ought to permit a barrier between oneself and another human being, no matter what differences there are of ideology or religion. There should be a continual dialogue going on.

"I've always," Muste continued, looking back, "tried to keep communication open between radicals and nonradicals, between pacifists and nonpacifists. It goes back to something very fundamental in the nonviolent approach to life. You always assume there is some element of truth in the position of the other person, and you respect your opponent for hanging on to an idea as long as he believes it to be true. On the other hand, you must try very hard to see what truth actually does exist in his idea, and seize on it to make him realize what you consider to be a larger truth.

"Action," Muste rose to indicate to his visitor that he had to return to work, "is the other part of the equation. You keep the lines of communication open, and you act on your own ideas."

Epilogue

In November, 1962, anthropologist Loren Eiseley wrote in *The New York Times Book Review* about Peter Matthiessen's *Under the Mountain Wall: A Chronicle of Two Seasons in the Stone Age*. Eiseley noted that implicit in Matthiessen's description of the primitive Kurelu was the fundamental resemblance between these savages and those who have been "civilized" throughout recorded time. "In those great tribes which constitute modern nations," Eiseley added, "many complications have arisen, but still the aggressive and powerful threaten and contend, brandishing unheard-of weapons across the breadth of seas; still the quiet go in fear of the violent, and women and children are afraid in the night. Our ways change but slowly if at all."

Matthiessen had written in his book of a Kurelu funeral ceremony: "In this dessicated thing they seemed to glimpse themselves, just for a moment; this was the way that all of them would go, under a blue sky, in a late twilight." Eiseley commented: "Perhaps in the long

252

atomic testing that wears out the lives of this, our primitive generation, there are those who think, even in weariness—this is the way we will all go, the evil, the good, the innocent, in a pillar of smoke at twilight, and the earth be no more troubled. . . ."

As A. J. Muste nears eighty, he continues with extraordinary energy and perseverance to battle against the possibility of this vision becoming actual.

In my own case—and I am a convert to nuclear pacifism—my exploration of A. J. Muste's life and ideas helped greatly to confirm that conversion. I came to believe, along with journalist I. F. Stone, that "when newspaper headlines begin to proclaim the coming of the incedible, the mystics begin to seem the only sober observers."

Not only the mystics, however. As I hope I have made clear, A. J. Muste, for example, is not a mystic except as that term applies to his private religion. In his long life, Muste has been as practical a radical as it was possible for him to be in that he has continually tested his principles in action.

Since his return to pacifism in 1936, the driving force in Muste's life has been quite literally an attempt to save the world as well as to change it. After Hiroshima, Muste has been joined by many more peace agitators than ever existed before in the history of American pacifism. He and they are still very much a minority, but increasingly, they are disturbing more of the unconverted with a problem in the semantics of survival. Who now are the realists?

"The demand," Muste insists, "that training for nuclear war be simply scrapped as irrational and indecent is not utopian. The realists today are the members of the San Francisco to Moscow Walk; the sitdowners in Trafalgar Square; those who have sailed on the

Golden Rule, the *Phoenix* and the three *Everyman* ships
—all who starkly pose this question and relentlessly and
nonviolently press this demand."

While never ingenuously optimistic, Muste continues
to refuse to be paralyzed by pessimism. As he once said,
"A Christian can never be a fatalist." That is, a Chris-
tain according to Muste's criteria of that faith. As for
myself, I have enormous doubts as to whether Muste
and others like him will ever reach enough people so
that the primitiveness of the way men rule and are
ruled is finally ended. It may well be too late to prevent
the obliteration of much of mankind in the "pillar of
smoke at twilight" described by Loren Eiseley. Muste,
however, will continue to act in the fierce belief that so
long as there is life, the forces of death—however they
are euphemized and disguised by the rulers and nearly
all of the ruled—must be resisted.

The essence of A. J. Muste's character and life is of
the same vein as that insight into himself noted by
Thoreau in his essay on civil disobedience. Writing of
the night he was imprisoned for nonpayment of a tax
to support the Mexican War, Thoreau said, "I saw that,
if there was a wall of stone between me and my towns-
men, there was a still more difficult one to climb or
break through before they could get to be as free as
I was."

INDEX

American Society of Friends, Muste on, 200; Philadelphia yearly meeting of 1961, 175

American Third Camp Committee, 140

American Woolen Company Mills, and Muste, 53

American Workers Party, 88, 140; absorbs C.P.L.A., 88-89; and Workers Party of the U.S., 90

Anti-Semitism, Muste on, 193-196

Arizona State University, 214

Atheism, Muste on, 188

Auden, W. H., 34

Auto-Lite strike, in Toledo, Ohio, 86

Ayusawa, Iwao, tribute to Muste, 11

Baker, Nancy (née Muste), quoted on family, 142-143. *See also* Muste, Nancy

Baldwin, Roger, on Lawrence strike, 54-55; and Muste, 115-116, 165-166; on Muste in Africa, 203

Baldwin Mills, Marion, N.C., strikes at, 77-78

Baptist Church peace fellowship, 178

Barry, Joseph, on Muste, 215

Beard, Charles, 74

Beecher, John, joins San Francisco to Moscow Peace Walkers, 214

Beirut, Lebanon, World Peace Brigade meeting at, 220-221

Bell, Tartt, on Muste, 208

Benét, Stephen Vincent, 63

Bennett, James, 122

Bhave, Vinoba, sponsors World Peace Brigade, 220

Bigelow, Albert, and voyage of *Golden Rule,* 152-154

Blumberg, Albert, 167

Bolshoi Ballet, 247

Bondurant, Joan V., 233

Boston University School of Theology, 13

Bradley, General Omar, on nuclear deterrence, 136

Brethren, 138

Brethren Church, 10

Brick, Allan, and Muste, 208-210

Bristol, James, on Muste, 63-64; on Muste and F.O.R., 106

British Campaign for Nuclear Disarmament, sponsors *Everyman III* cruise, 225

Brock, Hugh, on Muste, 205

Bromley, Ernest, quoted, 206

Bromley, Marion, 206-207

Brooklyn College, civil defense protests at, 246

Brookwood Labor College, 8-9, 38, 141, 190; and American Federation of Labor, 59; and American Fund for Public Service, 60; and C.P.L.A., 77; and Muste, 80, 81-84; Muste an Educational Director of, 58-72

Brown, Bill, 100

Brown, John, 27

Buber, Martin, 182; sponsors World Peace Brigade, 220

Budenz, Louis, defects to Communist Party, 93; and Muste, 85-86

Buttrick, George H., 179

Calvinism, 28, 98

Camus, Albert, *Neither Victims Nor Executioners,* 195

Cannon, James, 86; and Muste, 89-90, 91-92; and Trotsky, 90